# THE ART AND CRAFT OF WOOD

Woodworking can be a dangerous activity. Failure to follow safety procedures may result in serious injury or death. This book provides useful instruction, but we cannot anticipate all of your working conditions or the characteristics of your materials and tools. For your safety, you should use caution, care, and good judgment when following the procedures described in this book. Consider your own skill level and the instructions and safety precautions associated with the various tools and materials shown. The publisher cannot assume responsibility for any damage to property or injury to persons as a result of misuse of the information provided.

Quarto is the authority on a wide range of topics.
Quarto educates, entertains and enriches the lives of our readers—enthusiasts and lovers of hands-on living.
www.QuartoKnows.com

© 2017 Quarto Publishing Group USA, Inc.
Text © 2017 Tiny Chair Pictures, LLC
Photography © 2017 Tiny Chair Pictures, LLC

First published in the United States of America in 2017 by
Quarry Books, an imprint of
The Quarto Group
100 Cummings Center
Suite 265-D
Beverly, Massachusetts 01915-6101
Telephone: (978) 282-9590
Fax: (978) 283-2742
QuartoKnows.com
Visit our blogs at QuartoKnows.com

Quarry Books titles are also available at discount for retail, wholesale, promotional, and bulk purchase. For details, contact the Special Sales Manager by email at specialsales@quarto.com or by mail at The Quarto Group, Attn: Special Sales Manager, 401 Second Avenue North, Suite 310, Minneapolis, MN 55401, USA.

10 9 8 7 6 5 4 3 2 1

ISBN: 978-1-63159-297-3

Digital edition published in 2017

Library of Congress Cataloging-in-Publication Data is available.

Design: Paul Burgess at Burge Agency
Artwork: Archie Strong at Burge Agency
Photography: Tiny Chair Pictures, LLC

Printed in China

# THE ART AND CRAFT OF WOOD

A PRACTICAL GUIDE TO HARVESTING, CHOOSING, RECLAIMING, PREPARING, CRAFTING, AND BUILDING WITH RAW WOOD

- SILAS J KYLER & DAVID HILDRETH -

QUARRY

# CONTENTS

**PART ONE**

## CHOOSING WOOD FOR YOUR PROJECT

**PART TWO**

## MILLING AND SEASONING

# INTRODUCTION

Makers of all kinds know the incredible rewards of creating something with their own hands. Regardless the medium—wood, fabric, metal, clay, concrete, glass—designing, creating, and building something yourself feels good. What if this feeling didn't only come from the end product, but came from the creation and processing of the building material itself? A common trait of makers is the ongoing and ever deepening appreciation for the raw materials they are using. As filmmakers and authors, we seek to create pieces with intrinsic value from the materials right through to the finished product.

We have also come to discover this joy of production working with raw wood. One hot summer in Arizona, we came across a storm-downed tree in someone's front yard. This tree, in this moment, was begging to be something more. We managed to save the tree from the landfill and began a journey to fully transform it. In fact, we became so inspired by this idea that we made a documentary film about it.

We had the two-ton (1,814 kg) log hauled off the driveway where it had come crashing down. We found a sawmill in the heart of our busy city. We did our best to dry the wood without it warping. We flattened the wonky boards with a homemade router jig and then flattened them again when they continued to warp. We called in favors to help plane and sand the wood. We designed two tables and finally got to work putting them together.

Before we came along, the log was being cut up into chunks to be thrown piece by piece into a landfill. With this book, you will see pieces of art others don't see. What another person may view as a worthless dead tree, you will see an opportunity to make something great. It is a huge undertaking and, honestly, we didn't exactly know what we were getting ourselves into. But when the sawdust settled, we had two incredible works of art that tell a story of redemption and display the value of hard work. That's what *The Art and Craft of Wood* is all about.

The hardest part of the process is deciding to go for it. Large tree trunks and even small limbs can be intimidating, and (not to discourage you . . . ) they

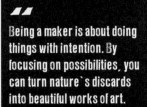

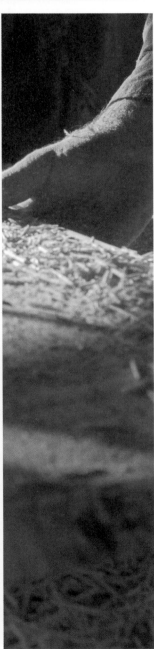

take an enormous amount of work to process. But why should it be easy? Being a maker is about doing things with intention. Through some hard work and resourcefulness, you can turn a log into a beautiful piece of furniture. It's not the easy way to make furniture, but you'll gain a sense of satisfaction from the labor of your hands, the skills you learn, and the connections you make in the process.

Being a maker is about doing things with intention. With hard work, you can turn trash into beautiful works of art.

Even though the process can be difficult and frustrating at times, it isn't rocket science. Like anything else, there are manageable steps to getting started. You don't have to choose the biggest log. You don't have to dive in with a major project, but you do have to dive in somewhere. This book addresses urban lumber, which is a term encompassing

lumber that is produced by individuals from trees that wouldn't normally be used as commercial lumber. Urban lumber comes from near where people live. We aren't talking about chopping down trees just to use for lumber. These are trees that have come down in a storm or must be removed because they are dead, dying, or unwanted.

Typically, when local trees are removed, they are chopped up by a tree removal company and never seen

again, often being dumped in a landfill or thrown into the chipper to become mulch. Urban lumber offers redemption to materials that still have use.

Isn't it a shame to see good materials wasted, especially something as beautiful as a tree? We love our neighborhood trees, but as soon as they stop standing upright, they are considered garbage. Every year, millions upon millions of tons of usable wood are thrown away. Most often they are put into the landfill where

they will slowly decompose, releasing all the carbon dioxide they were storing, or, somewhat better, tossed into a chipper to become mulch. Meanwhile, we are sold furniture made with lumber from halfway around the world, often harvested irresponsibly and resulting in deforestation. Every time someone redeems a tree to a higher purpose, it makes a statement that these trees are useful for more than mulch and that there is real value in good craftsmanship.

As we made *Felled*, a documentary film about giving new life to fallen urban trees, we traveled around the country and heard from lumber workers and artisans. Every one of them was excited to share about the rewards of their craft and the merits of experiencing the art of woodworking.

We will share our experiences and wisdom we've picked up along the way to help you build up some of the core skills required to create finished household

> If nothing else, we hope this book gives you the gumption to stare down the nearest log and make some sawdust.

Silas and James glue a table top together in the documentary film *Felled*.

The beauty of an acacia log is uncovered for the first time.

objects from raw wood. These skills will be imparted by means of practical projects ranging in difficulty from a beginner to intermediate level, all made from raw wood. Even if you don't have extensive shop experience, if you have a willingness to learn, ask questions, and fail, you are ready to tackle the projects in this book.

This book covers taking raw logs and milling useful lumber by yourself or with the help of a professional sawyer, using basic drying and flattening techniques to produce uniform boards, practicing basic joinery to fit the boards together, and developing the sanding and finishing skills to make your projects look their best. Lastly, we'll cover how to split and season firewood and various uses for wood waste.

You'll primarily read advice from Silas, who brings expertise not as a master woodworker, but as a filmmaker who has spent time with a lot of master woodworkers. He himself is a woodworking enthusiast who enjoys working with raw-wood in a home-shop environment. He'll share what he's picked up along the way from his experiences in a practical hands-on way. He knows what it's like to start from the beginning and the basic skills you'll need to get started.

Working with wood is fun, rewarding, and socially responsible. If nothing else, we hope this book gives you the gumption to stare down the nearest log and make some sawdust.

# THE TOOLS

In our consumer-driven environment, there is always the danger of over-emphasizing the tools over the craft. This happens often in the filmmaking world when new camera models come out and enthusiasts eagerly discuss what new features will be incorporated in the latest-and-greatest gear. Invariably, there is an initial excitement, then disappointment in the lack of such-and-such a feature, and they wait for the next model. Meanwhile, they'll use whatever tools are at their disposal to create content and tell stories. Woodworking is no different.

When shooting *Felled*, I toured the New Yankee Workshop with Norm Abram, an accomplished woodworker, and I remarked that the tools in his shop would sure make my life easier. His response was enlightening: "It's not the tools, it's the person behind the tools."

Even with a wide range of tools at your disposal, there will always be newer models with better features or even older, more durable models that you don't have access to. Many tools have a seemingly endless list of add-ons

and accessories. Every tool needs to be maintained and carefully sharpened. The more tools you have, the more easily the craft of woodworking can become the craft of working on your workshop and tools.

To avoid that issue, I suggest a project-oriented approach, where you choose tools and equipment based on your end goal. This approach is especially effective for a more casual enthusiast, requiring less time and a smaller budget. If it is any encouragement, humankind has been fashioning objects from wood since we have been in existence, using all manner of tools. Find solace in knowing that throughout history, amazing objects have been crafted with the simplest tools and few resources.

That is not to say that tools are not important. There are basic tasks that are required for successfully crafting a variety of wooden objects. In most cases, there are several tools that can accomplish the same task. With a little ingenuity, you can do a lot with only a few tools.

Thankfully, there are lots of ways to get access to tools. If you live in an area

with an active online sellers' community, that is hands-down the best place to find used tools to purchase for significantly less than brand new tools would cost. They don't make 'em like they used to, but thankfully, the ones they used to make are still available online.

If you don't have much of a space to work in or store tools, many cities have communal workspaces. These spaces are often called maker spaces, usually have a variety of tools for many disciplines beyond woodworking, and often have experts willing to give guidance. Another excellent option is taking a class at a community college or art center. Hands-on professional instruction in a well-equipped workshop can introduce you to new skills and tool options.

Finally, using your resources—like family, neighbors, and friends—is a great way to make the best use of tools. I constantly have people in my workshop creating their own projects with my tools. Creating is a joyous thing, and sharing that experience with others is a lot of fun as well, so take advantage of the community around you.

## WOODWORKING TASKS

**RIPPING:** Cutting lengthwise with the grain

**CROSSCUTTING:** Cutting across the grain

**BORING:** Hollowing out and making holes

**ROUTING:** Hollowing out, cutting grooves and curves, and creating edge patterns

**PLANING:** Removing thickness from the surface

**JOINTING:** Squaring and straightening board edges

**SMOOTHING:** Sanding or scraping

**JOINING:** Attaching pieces together

**FINISHING:** Sealing to enhance grain and protect wood

## THE TASKS

Though you're likely wondering what tools are essential for a beginner, there's no perfect answer to that question. Here is a look at a rough outline of any basic raw wood to final product woodworking project:

The log is hauled, milled, and seasoned.

Rough slabs of raw wood are sized to the desired width, length, and thickness.

Edges and faces are squared and leveled.

Material is added or removed to create individual parts and joinery.

Components are joined in assembly.

Surfaces are smoothed and polished.

The product is finished and sealed for beauty and longevity.

Each step requires a few specialized tools, but all require the same level of attention to detail and willingness to devote time and energy.

## THE TOOLS

There are many various combinations of tools that can perform the same list of essential functions, so let's outline some of the common tools along with some guidelines for selecting specific makes and models. Raw wood does add some additional complexity over the process of heading down to the hardwood store and picking up milled, flattened, and straightened lumber, but for the sake of this section, we will only deal with the tools required to get from rough lumber to finished piece, leaving the tools of gathering and milling logs in their respective sections.

## HAND TOOLS

**HANDSAWS**—Saws are available for every wood cutting application. The orientation of the teeth and structure of the blade and handle determine its uses. See the sidebar for our favorites.

**CHISELS**—Available in a variety of sizes and shapes, these hand tools with beveled blades are used for wood shaping.

**WOODEN MALLET**—This is used to drive chisels and gently tap parts into place.

**HAND PLANE**—This tool is made to remove materials from and flatten the face of the board and adjust thickness. There are many specialized variations for a wide variety of tasks.

**CLAMPS**—These are used to push or pull parts together. Bar, pipe, hand screw, and C clamps are the most common in the woodworking shop.

**COMBINATION SQUARE**—A square is used to determine if edges are at right angles, or square. This one combines a ruler and square for a handy reference.

**TRY SQUARE**—This is used to determine if a surface is square or a joint is at right angles.

**CARPENTER'S SQUARE**—This is a metal square with long legs usually marked with a ruler. It is very versatile, especially when working with large slabs.

**LEVEL**—This is a tool designed to determine how horizontal (level) or vertical (plumb) a surface is. It can be used as a straightedge cutting guide for hand tools when needed.

**RULER**—This is a short strip of metal with accurate length markings for measuring.

**MEASURING TAPE**—This is a retractable measuring device.

**BEVEL GAUGE**—This is an adjustable gauge for setting and transferring angles.

**SANDING BLOCK**—This is a block of wood or rubber to which a piece of sandpaper is affixed.

**SCREWDRIVER**—This tool is used to drive screws. It is available with a number of blades, most typically flat and Phillips.

**MOISTURE METER**—This is a handheld device calibrated to measure the moisture content of lumber.

# HANDSAWS

You could own dozens of saws because there is one for every cutting situation. Here are some favorites:

**PANEL SAW**—This was named such because it could fit in the panel of a work chest. It is also called a carpenter's saw and is what people most commonly think of when thinking of a handsaw. It has a large easy-to-grip wood handle with a blade about 20 inches (51 cm) long and teeth configured for ripping or crosscutting boards to rough dimensions. There are also combination options available.

**MITER SAW**—This is a saw with a special stand or box for cutting boards to length at precise angles. The saw itself usually has a reinforced top edge for rigidity.

**FLUSH CUT PULL SAW**—This is a Japanese-inspired tool with a thin flexible blade for making very fine cuts in wood and the ability to cut flush with a surface. Unlike most saws, it cuts on the pull stroke, not the push.

**COPING SAW**—This has a small U-shaped body with thin removable blades for cutting intricate shapes and curves. The blade can be removed, threaded through a hole, and reattached to make interior cuts.

## HANDHELD POWER TOOLS

**CIRCULAR SAW**—This is a power saw that rapidly spins a round blade with teeth for both ripping and crosscutting. Sometimes referred to by the brand name SKILSAW, it's a versatile tool, especially when used in conjunction with a track or straight edge. It is available in a wide range of blade sizes, motor power, and prices.

**POWER DRILL**—This is used for boring holes into wood by driving removable drill bits. It is also used for driving screws and is available as corded (more powerful) and cordless (more portable).

**ROUTER**—This is a high-speed motor with removable cutting heads designed for hollowing out material from the surface of the wood. Routers can be equipped with interchangeable bases for freehand or fixed use. The cutting heads, called router bits, are available in a vast array of configurations.

**RANDOM ORBIT SANDER**—This is a power sander that moves the sandpaper in an irregular circular pattern at high speed.

**BISCUIT JOINER**—This is a specialty tool that cuts small slots in board edges to hold biscuits for joining pieces of wood. It is most often used for gluing up larger panels.

**BELT SANDER**—This is a powerful tool that drives a belt of sandpaper mounted on two drums. It removes surface material quickly and is usually reserved for tasks like rough shaping and flattening table tops.

**POWER PLANER**—This has special cutting heads for removing material from a board's surface. It is more similar to the stand-alone power planer than to the manual hand planer.

**JIGSAW**—This is a handheld reciprocating saw with a short and straight blade for cutting curved shapes in wood.

## STANDALONE POWER TOOLS

**TABLE SAW**—This is a powerful circular saw mounted under a table. The blade can be raised, lowered, or angled. A variety of blade options allows for ripping, crosscutting, and dado cutting. The table has features that allow for precision cutting with fences, sleds, and miter gauges. This tool is very versatile, is one of the most common tools in woodworking shops, and is available in any size or price range.

**MITER SAW**—Similar in purpose to its hand-powered cousin, this saw uses a circular blade to cut boards to length and can be set to precise angles. Compound miter saws can cut miter angles in two axes simultaneously.

**SURFACE PLANER**—This has a large drum-shaped cutting head with 3 long straight cutters that evenly remove material across the entire surface of a board. The board rides on a flat metal bed and is driven along by two power rollers, which help keep the material from shifting during the cutting process. It is available in many sizes and prices.

**BANDSAW**—This consists of a long, thin looped saw blade running vertically through guides driven by two large drive wheels. The workpiece rests a table with an opening for the blade to pass through and is moved along this table throughout the cut. It is good for cutting slabs off small logs, cutting boards on edge, and cutting irregular shapes such as curves very smoothly.

**JOINTER**—A cutting head set between two beds, which are offset in elevation, takes material off the face or edge of a board. It is useful for flattening, squaring, and straightening boards.

**ROUTER TABLE**—This is a specially made table with an adjustable guide fence and miter slot for mounting a router upside down with the bit extended beyond the table's surface. It makes the router even more versatile for any number of hollowing tasks and routing tasks.

**DRILL PRESS**—This is a stationary machine for precision drilling.

**BENCH SANDER**—This is a combination belt and disc sander with adjustable tables for shaping and smoothing.

# THE WORKBENCH

You will need at least one flat, stable surface to work on. Some woodworkers emphasize the workbench as the heart of their shop, often spending many hours crafting their own or thousands of dollars purchasing one. Indeed, there is something satisfying about a sturdily built, well thought-out workbench. I have personally never found the time to design and build one of my own and don't have the budget to purchase one of high caliber. The one I have now came from my mom's old place, probably cost a couple hundred dollars new, and to be honest, isn't that great. It wobbles a bit when I try to plane something by hand, and its clamps are of relatively poor quality, but I haven't replaced the bench yet because it isn't holding me back. It gets the job done and fits the bill for my work. That's the key to choosing a work surface of your own; choose something that lets you do what you need to do without holding you back.

The requirements for any workbench are that it be relatively flat, have enough space to lay out what you're building, and easily allow for clamping of workpieces. Tour a variety of shops and you will see a variety of workbenches, from as simple as a door lying flat between two sawhorses to huge 300 pound (136 kg) handcrafted maple benches with built-in clamps. Out of these shops comes the same level of beautiful craftsmanship, with each craftsman having come to have their own work style. When starting out, you don't know the way you work best, so I would begin with something as basic and inexpensive as possible until you have a better idea of what you need in your workbench. There are many plans readily available for building your own bench if that is something that appeals to you.

# DUST COLLECTION

There is no way to escape the fact that this activity produces a copious amount of sawdust. As you build your tool collection, you need to consider how to collect and dispose of the dust you are creating. There are both practical and health reasons for this. In the section about safety, we talk about the health implications of sawdust and how to protect yourself, but as far as practicality, having all that dust piling up is a major nuisance. Also, many tools like planers and routers will have very poor performance, if they work at all, without some form of dust collection.

The first dust collection machine an enthusiast will own is typically a shop vacuum. These are quite effective for many tools, especially smaller tools like hand sanders or router tables. However, larger tools, such as planers and the like, may eventually require the purchase of a purpose-built dust collector. When researching tools, consider selecting models that have dust collection ports built-in.

# BEGINNER'S WORKSHOP CHECKLIST

When first starting out, a powerful, yet inexpensive combination of tools would be as follows:

- ☐ Inexpensive workbench
- ☐ Entry-level table saw or handheld circular saw
- ☐ Power miter saw
- ☐ Handheld power jigsaw
- ☐ Power drill
- ☐ Plunge router
- ☐ Flush cut pull saw
- ☐ Random orbit sander
- ☐ Hand plane
- ☐ Chisels (¼", ½", ¾" [6, 13, 19 mm])
- ☐ Metal ruler, try square, carpenter square, and measuring tape
- ☐ Straight edge
- ☐ 4 to 8 bar clamps 12 to 24" (30.5 to 61 cm) long
- ☐ Shop vacuum

With these tools, you would be able to build all the projects in this book, with some exceptions. Without a bandsaw, you wouldn't be able to mill any small logs yourself, and any planing work beyond what you could accomplish with a hand plane would need to be taken to a commercial planer. The reason I left out the bandsaw and planer is they tend to have a higher price of entry than many of the more common tools. If budget allows, these would be valuable additions to your workshop. Without these two, a group of tools such as this could be pulled together for a few hundred dollars by trolling through classified ads and sellers' forums and waiting for the right deals to come along.

Talk to other woodworkers and they will all have their own opinions and advice on which tools are most valuable when starting out. All are equally valid because of the highly personal and flexible nature of the hobby. There are woodworkers who exclusively use good ol' fashioned hand tools and produce work that blows mine out of the water. There is more than one road to follow.

For most every woodworker, the excitement of getting a new tool can be addictive. There's something magical about putting a new tool to use for the first time and being able to expand your woodworking horizons with it. Later in this book, we will discuss the specific tools you need for each project, from splitting a log to joining two boards together. Don't worry too much if you don't have all the tools you'd like or think you may need; simply take it a project at a time and before you know it, you'll find yourself with a growing collection of tools and the skills to use them.

# SAFETY CONSIDERATIONS

Working with raw wood holds its fair share of hazards. Throughout this book, we will discuss the use of various tools—tools that can be hazardous if you aren't careful. If it cuts wood, it can certainly cut you. We will also talk about moving logs that may be large and heavy, which can be a dangerous task. Before diving into the hands-on portions of the book, it is prudent for us explain the dangers and how to avoid them just as an experienced woodworker would do in the shop when instructing a novice.

## UNDERSTANDING THE RISKS

The most common issues that arise from these hazards can be broken into two main categories: acute and chronic. The Occupational Safety and Health Administration (OSHA) refers to problems causing immediate injuries as safety hazards, such as saw cuts, kickback, and flying woodchips. Long-term risks are described as health hazards caused by exposure to dust, loud noise, vibrations, and chemicals. Immediate harm can come from improper exposure to dust through an allergic reaction or asthma attack,

and chemical exposure can also have immediate impact, so the lines between safety hazards and health hazards can be a bit blurry. Health professionals use these terms, so they are helpful to understand if you do have an injury.

My friend Todd, a local sawyer who moves heavy logs daily, can attest to the dangers of this activity. He has had his fair share of injuries, including a broken collar bone from a log-propelled cant hook, a broken toe from a rolling log, and innumerable scrapes and bruises. Thankfully, he's avoided some of the more serious injuries that can occur, like crushed and broken appendages and head injuries. With the knowledge that he has gained the hard way, he can help others avoid these same issues. Having someone with experience to teach or assist you is invaluable.

## SHARP, ROTATING PARTS

Power tools use motors that drive blades and bits either directly or indirectly through a belt. It is important to avoid contact with sharp, rotating blades but also with the rotational movement. Drive wheels and belts can pinch, severing fingers or worse. A rotating bit will quickly grab and pull loose fabric or hair,

so it's important to keep long hair up, avoid baggy clothing, and never wear gloves or long hanging jewelry when working in the workshop with power tools.

## KICKBACK

Beyond direct contact with machinery are the hazards posed by kickback. This is the most common cause of woodworking injury. Kickback occurs when the blade becomes bound or jammed in the workpiece being cut. The power of the machine suddenly and violently hurls the board back toward you. Dull blades, warped boards, and letting go of the workpiece are some common causes for kickback. Handheld power tools are prone to kick back as well, but often it's the tool trying to kick back rather than the workpiece. In general, there are a few good practices that can greatly reduce the chance of kickback:

Never leave an unattended board in contact with moving machinery, even for a fraction of a second.

Avoid cutting boards that do not have a straight edge.

Choose the appropriate tool for the job.

Maintain your tools and keep blades sharp.

Blades can be taken to professional sharpeners or replaced when necessary, and most equipment manuals have straightforward instructions on proper maintenance procedures specific to the tool.

## WOOD CHIPS AND DUST

The risk of small wood chips and dust flying into your eye is very real. Usually, this causes only temporary discomfort, but the side effects of reaching for your eye while using a power tool can be much more unpleasant. Wearing appropriate eye protection, such as safety glasses or a full face shield, is a simple but powerful safety procedure.

Some injuries occur over time. Lung and skin problems caused by dust exposure usually don't happen overnight, but stick at this hobby for a while without taking the proper precautions and they will make themselves known. Especially dangerous is long term dust exposure, which can cause problems like shortness of breath due to decreased lung capacity and can even potentially lead to cancer. Thankfully, simply wearing a basic respirator for dusty tasks virtually eliminates these problems.

## NOISE

Another hazard over the long term is potential hearing loss from using loud power tools. Wear earplugs or muff style protectors to diminish prolonged exposure to loud noises.

## ALLERGENS

Besides the long-term effects of excess dust exposure, there are other potential impacts to be aware of. Some time ago, I met a fellow who had a passion for woodturning. For years, he handcrafted beautiful bowls from many various types of wood. One day he was working with a piece of cherry wood and suddenly couldn't breathe right. It turns out he had developed an allergy to cherry wood; he became sick and was no longer able to tolerate wood dust at all. Years later, he could pick the hobby back up, but to this day avoids cherry. Having learned his lesson, he is careful to protect his lungs now by wearing a respirator while woodworking. People can develop wood allergies overnight, after which the body becomes very sensitive to even a small amount. Problems will typically manifest through difficulty breathing or a skin rash. Some woods, like walnut, are more likely to cause a reaction than others, but it's best to know how to protect yourself from all of them.

# BEST PRACTICES

I have a small workshop that is often in a state of transformation—in other words, it's a giant mess. I tell myself that it's part of my process. Whether the shop is a disaster or not, I always follow some basic practices when working, like keeping a clear space in my work area. This is one of many good general workshop practices that reduces the number of possible accidents.

Here is a list of ground rules to follow to maintain a safe working environment:

| |
|---|
| Keep the workspace and floor clear. |
| Maintain and inspect tools regularly. |
| Keep bits and blades sharp. |
| Unplug tools when changing or maintaining blades. |
| Ensure the tool is in the off position before plugging it in. |
| Use tools only for their designed function. |
| Don't wear gloves when operating machinery in the workshop . |
| Leave all safety guards in place whenever possible. |
| Never cut freehand on machines designed to be used with a fence. |
| Don't attempt to cut pieces too small or large for the tool. |
| Let the blade or bit reach maximum speed before beginning to cut. |
| Use a push stick whenever possible. |
| Never reach over a moving blade. |
| Keep the work area well ventilated. |
| Spread used finishing rags out to dry, never pile them up. |

## USE THE RIGHT TOOL

There are plenty of procedural methods of avoiding well-known woodworking hazards. Many are simple common sense. Using the wrong tool for the job is a classic mistake in the workshop. It's tempting to save time by avoiding another machine setup, but you are more likely to mess up your project, or worse, sustain an injury. Even if you don't have the right tool for the job, you can usually find a workaround, like building a jig to adapt your tool to the task or adapting your project to the tools you have access to.

## KNOW HOW TO USE THE TOOL SAFELY

Speaking of using the right tools, let's talk about the tools' safety features. Sometimes, you will see old-school woodworkers removing many guards from their tools. This is dangerous and not recommended, especially for a novice woodworker. People with years of practice know the risks and are often a couple of fingers short. A classic example is the table saw splitter. This simple device prevents most kickback scenarios, but many insist on removing it as soon as they set up their saw. Sometimes, a guard must be taken off for a specific operation, in which case it should be replaced before moving on to something else. Guards exist for a reason—to keep you safe.

## USE WOOD THAT IS THE PROPER SIZE

Later in the book we will talk about preparing material to use with various machinery. Know that you can't simply grab any piece of raw wood and immediately begin feeding it through the nearest power tool. First, wood must be examined for warpage and prepared with at least one (usually two) flat reference surfaces before it is safe to use. Ignore this and you could end up with some nasty kickback. In addition, it is important to understand that it is unsafe to use a piece of wood that is too large to properly support during a cut. Likewise, trying to cut a piece that is too short or narrow for a tool, leaving it without enough support, can result in flying chunks of wood or your hand too close to the blade. Always keep boards securely in place throughout the cut. Their length may require you to choose a different tool, while other times simply an additional support accessory or custom jig will get the job done. You must be willing to walk away from the cut until you are properly equipped to make it.

## BE AWARE OF BODY PLACEMENT

Proper body placement is very important to avoid slipping into moving blades or being in the path of flying kickback. The proper stance for every machine may be slightly different, but in general, make sure you are in position to maintain balance, not leaning into a blade. If your hand were to slip, the weight of your body should never be behind it in such a way as to force it into the machinery. To be out of harm's way of kickback, simply stand slightly off-axis from the direction of the blade, but not so far as to impede your balance.

Perhaps this goes without saying, but your fingers shouldn't get anywhere near the blade. I've seen some woodworkers brazenly placing hands in risky spots. Using a push stick, especially at the end of a cut, is a basic safety measure that advanced woodworkers often ignore—but you shouldn't.

## MONITOR THE MACHINE YOU'RE USING

It's important to listen to your machines as you use them. If you turn something on and there's an unusual amount of vibration, turn it off and inspect it thoroughly. During a cut, it's important not to force anything. Sometimes, you may hear the motor bogging down, or the material may become more difficult to feed. Usually, this means you need to slow down. If the workpiece becomes stuck, let the blade come to a complete stop before removing your hand; otherwise, it is very likely to result in kickback.

## PRACTICE PROPER DISPOSAL

We will not be spending a lot of time on various finishing methods in this book, but there is one critical instruction that cannot be ignored. When using any oil-based finish, it is critical to properly dispose of the used rags afterwards. To avoid spontaneous combustion, never leave saturated rags in a pile to dry. Rather, hang them up or lay them flat, ideally outside, allowing them to dry without building up heat.

## KNOW YOUR TOOLS

You must know and respect your tools. Power tools pack an incredible amount of power in a small package. Respect is different than fear. When you fear your tools, you become timid, holding back where confidence is needed. Knowledge overcomes fear, so become knowledgeable. Before you use any tool, take the necessary time to understand its operation and follow the instructions given in the operation manuals. If you aren't sure about a tool you are about to use or it makes you nervous in any way, pause. Step back, assess the situation, and find someone more experienced than you to give you some pointers. Here is a quick overview of the specific risks and functions of the most common woodworking tools.

### CHAINSAW

The gas chainsaw tops the list of dangerous tools used in this book because they are powerful handheld machines with large exposed blades. Electric chainsaws can be equally as dangerous, but most models do have significantly less power, with lower chain velocities than their gas-powered brethren. Chainsaw accidents are often the most severe. They're not exactly delicate tools. Used to slice through entire tree trunks with ease, it is no surprise that the average chainsaws can cause injuries resulting in hundreds of stitches or worse. Most often, these injuries occur to the legs and feet when the saw catches and lurches out of control.

The biggest danger from the chainsaw is when it becomes uncontrolled due to binding. Cuts should be carefully planned to avoid pinching the chain. The log being cut must be properly supported to avoid cutting into the ground and to prevent shifting during a cut.

Always operate a chainsaw as follows:

- At or below shoulder level
- Using both hands
- While maintaining sure footing

It would be wise to avoid using a chainsaw, especially for milling operations, until you have proper instruction and can operate it confidently and competently. Work deliberately and cautiously, only picking up speed as you grow into the experience. This goes for every tool, but especially the chainsaw. Use the appropriate safety gear, including chainsaw chaps, face shields, earmuffs, and steel-toe boots.

### TABLE SAW

Table saws are the most common tool in a woodworking shop and are responsible for the most injuries of any woodshop tool. For general woodworking, use a combination ripping/crosscutting blade and always keep the blade sharp. When setting the height of the blade, make sure the teeth clear the piece you are cutting unless you are making a blind cut. To avoid a kickback injury, stand to the side of the blade a bit and always use the supplied splitter. Never attempt to cut free-hand with a table saw; use the rip fence, a crosscut sled, or a miter gauge. Also, make sure the work piece has at least one face flat to ride on the table and a straight side to guide along the fence. Always use a push stick when pushing stock past the blade and ensure the cut has been completed and the workpiece is all the way past the saw before releasing pressure. If ripping a long board, make sure you support both ends with roller stands or table extensions.

## MITER SAW

A power miter saw is also a relatively safe tool. The workpiece should be firmly pressed up against the fence. Do not attempt to cut a piece of wood too short to clamp to the table. When adjusting the miter angle, make sure the angle lock is secured in place. Do not begin the downward cut before the blade has reached maximum speed. Cut with a smooth steady motion, not too slow or rushed. When you complete the cut, allow the blade to stop completely before raising it.

## BANDSAW

The biggest cause of injury with the bandsaw is inattention to hand or finger location. To keep the blade from being overly stressed and possibly breaking, always choose the appropriate blade for the task. The wider the blade, the less tight a curve it can cut; forcing it will cause too much stress on the blade. Always be aware of where your fingers are and when necessary, use a push stick to complete a cut.

## PLANER

The planer removes material from the surface using a cylindrical cutting head and feeding the material through using its own built-in power feeders. You should always place yourself to the side of the bed and never put your hands closer than 3 inches (8 cm) of the infeed or outfeed. Avoid feeding boards with loose pieces. Boards shorter than 12 inches (30.5 cm) or the distance between the feed rollers should not be fed through the planer.

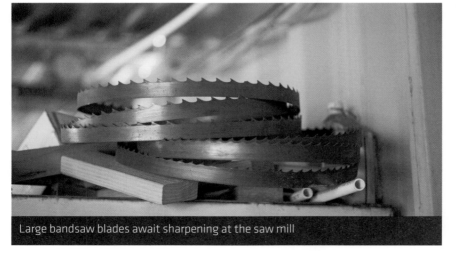

Large bandsaw blades await sharpening at the saw mill

## JOINTER

The jointer uses the same kind of cylindrical head as the planer. Operation is quite different, however, as are the safety requirements. When using the jointer, it is important to keep your hands at least 6 inches (15 cm) away from the head by using push blocks and paddles. Material less than 12 inches (30.5 cm) long should be avoided, and never run material on its face that's less than 1/2-inch (13 mm) thick. To avoid kickback, take small passes, preferably around 1/32 of an inch (0.8 mm). Like most machines, stand to the side, not in the direction that kickback would occur. If the jointer doesn't have a functioning spring loaded safety guard, do not use it.

## DRILL PRESS AND HANDHELD DRILL

Invaluable tools, drills used with wood are relatively safe, but care must still be taken. Always secure small workpieces to keep your hands out of harm's way. The larger the bit diameter, the more torque it generates when contacting the material, so it's important to keep the bit spinning at the appropriate speed for the material and avoid shifting the bit's angle while drilling to keep it from catching and twisting the workpiece or your wrist (when using a hand drill).

## ROUTER AND ROUTER TABLE

Routers can be operated as handheld tools or installed into a router table. The bits spin extremely fast (up to 24,000 RPM), so if you notice any odd vibrations, turn the router off immediately and investigate. Clean and inspect the collets to see if worn parts or dirt is causing the bit to be slightly skewed. Only use bits specifically designed for use in routers, and for some larger bits, you must have a variable speed router to be able to spin the bit at a lower RPM. Always follow the manufacturer's recommendations for any bit used. It is important to leave around 1/16 of an inch (1.5 mm) between the bottom of mounting collet and the router bit; otherwise, it could loosen during operation.

Your workpiece should be well secured, and when operating the router by hand and routing along an edge, you should always move left to right or counterclockwise, which is the opposite direction the bit is turning. When using the router table, always keep the bit inside the fence; do not run a workpiece in between the bit and fence. The result of such could be nasty kickback. As always, it is important to keep your hands safe, so when pushing stock through a table, use a push stick, or miter gauge when applicable, to keep hands and bit well apart.

## CIRCULAR SAW

Typically, kickback on a circular saw will cause the saw to jump rather than the workpiece. Models with a splitting knife are much better at avoiding this than those without. Ensure that the blade is set to the proper depth, teeth extending beyond the workpiece, and be aware of what is underneath to avoid cutting into something unintentionally. Smaller boards must be well secured prior to cutting. Large pieces must be well supported—including the waste piece. Keeping both hands on the saw keeps your fingers safe. Sorry, lefties—these saws are designed for righties, so extra care must be given when operating with your left hand.

## BELT SANDER

Keep far away from the drive belt during operation. A guard should be over the belt areas as well. When sanding freehand on corners, keep the workpiece angled down slightly in the direction of the sanding belt rotation for proper control. Always control the workpiece when in contact with the sandpaper, whether using the support table or not. Special care must be given when sanding small pieces, and if too small, a backing block should be used to keep a buffer between the workpiece and sander. Sanders create a lot of fine dust; wear your dust mask or respirator and when possible, capture as much of the dust as you can with a shop vacuum or specialized dust collection vacuum.

## HAND TOOLS

Hand tools are generally less likely to cause major injuries. An injury will typically occur to the nondominant hand due to poor placement as well as improperly driving the tool with the dominant hand. Sometimes, you'll want to put all your strength behind a tool, but care must be taken to keep control if the blade suddenly becomes loose. Never put your nondominant hand behind the blade in the direction you are pushing lest you lose control. The best defense against accidents with hand tools is to keep the blades sharp. Similar to a kitchen knife, a dull blade is much more dangerous, as it requires more force to do the same job.

## SAFETY GEAR

Thankfully, for basic woodworking in the workshop there aren't a lot of pieces of safety gear required. Three simple pieces of safety gear make a world of difference: ear protection, dust mask, and eye protection. Beyond these, avoid loose or baggy clothing, loose long hair, or any hanging jewelry like bracelets or necklaces as they can become tangled with a tool blade, drawing you toward the blade. Long pants and long sleeve shirts can help keep dust off the skin if generating a lot of dust but are a matter of preference. When working with logs, a minimum of protective chaps and sturdy footwear are necessary.

## EAR PROTECTION

Simple foam earplugs will work, but beyond infrequent use, they can be a nuisance. Consider some over-ear earmuffs; they are more comfortable to wear for a long period, are quick to take on and off, and last a long time. You can even find them with built in headphones to listen to some sweet beats while you work. Don't be that guy that needs his grandkid to repeat every other word.

## DUST MASK

Protecting your lungs should be a top priority. For quick operations that aren't too dusty, disposable dust masks with the adjustable metal clip over the bridge of your nose are decently effective. However, if you have an allergy to a specific type of wood dust or are doing something very dusty for a longer period, those masks only filter out 95 percent of the fine particles; they are simply limiting your exposure. For more serious work, get a half facemask reusable respirator with replaceable filters. This option is more comfortable to wear and is more effective for long-term use.

Note that if you are using any sort of chemical that releases harmful fumes, you must use a respirator with the appropriate filters. Disposable face masks won't block out those fumes.

## EYE PROTECTION

A basic set of safety glasses will protect against most woodchips and other flying debris that may come shooting toward your eyes. If using a chainsaw mill, or other task that creates a lot of flying pieces, a full face shield is invaluable. Even the smallest irritant can distract you and cause a major slipup.

## SAFETY CHAPS

Chainsaw injuries typically happen to the lower extremities. To address that risk, you can find protective chaps that upon contact will almost instantly jam the chain, minimizing any possible contact with flesh. Beyond the use of a low power electric chainsaw, these chaps are a necessity.

## STURDY FOOTWEAR

When selecting footwear, make sure they allow for good grip and ankle support. For protection against shifting logs, a good pair of steel-toe boots is highly recommended. There's no substitute for sure footing as anyone who has ever moved a large log will tell you.

## KNOW YOURSELF

Having understood some of the potential risks out there, and the ways to protect yourself from them, you are almost ready to roll up your sleeves and begin. To close this safety introduction out, I want to leave you with some final thoughts on the matter.

Know your limits and take care of yourself. Mistakes happen most often when people are tired, lose focus, or are rushing. You know yourself, so listen to your body and make a conscious decision to stop working before the point things become dangerous. If you do something enough times, there's a danger of becoming complacent and losing proper attention to detail. Develop your own routines with safety checks built-in. Getting those important details to become habit can save you a lot of grief down the road. Trying to speed through a task is one of the worst things you can do. Let's remember that this is supposed to be enjoyable as we work. When tempted to rush, take a deep breath and purposely slow down.

## CHECK IN WITH YOUR INTUITION

Check in with your gut, so to speak. If your next action doesn't pass a gut-check, don't continue. Use common sense to judge risk. Perhaps this is an overly-conservative approach, but it's always been a rule I've followed myself, and it's served me well thus far. If nothing else, the added time spent considering what you are about to do can only improve your understanding, allowing you to work with confidence. A sure, steady hand makes a world of difference.

My hope is that these descriptions of safety hazards do not turn you off from working with wood altogether. I don't want to minimize the risks, but the good news is that you can take many simple precautions to protect yourself. You will see safety tips and reminders throughout the book reminding you of these best practices. Despite the inherent risks of woodworking, it is a gratifying hobby with beautiful results.

# PART ONE

# CHOOSING WOOD FOR YOUR PROJECT

An Aleppo pine log being milled.

# IDENTIFYING AND SOURCING WOOD

In making *Felled*, we talked with a lot of people who work with raw wood. Each of them had their own reasons for doing so, but the common link between them was that they appreciated that wood could tell a narrative. People love stories. As one sawyer told me, "Inside a tree is a history of the life that plant led. What you see when you look inside is a piece of wood telling its own story of what it was like for it to be alive."

Perhaps this is a helpful perspective for you as you set out to find some raw wood for your next project. Look for unique pieces of wood with interesting sources. For example, maybe there is a fruit orchard near you that has been a longstanding staple of the community. Contact the owner and ask if they have any old trees they need to remove. Or perhaps you find a beloved neighborhood tree that has blown over in a windstorm. Get permission to make something with the wood. Just knowing where the tree came from, and having your hand in what it becomes, is a major advantage of working with raw wood. When selecting your material, you'll need to know the following:

Where to find raw wod

How to identify the wood

If the wood is suitable for your project

## SOURCING RAW WOOD

Whether you live in a rural area or in the middle of a big city, you will find trees around you. Like any living thing, trees have a limited lifespan and are constantly being planted and dying, so there will always be sources for raw wood. We are not cutting down healthy trees for lumber, but repurposing what is already being removed.

Cleaning an inclusion in an urban black acacia log. City trees are often full of unique features like these, where irregular growing conditions or damage causes pockets of bark to be enveloped by the tree as it grows, waiting to be found.

## WHERE TO SOURCE TREES

Your property

Property of neighbors, family, or friends (with permission)

Tree services

Green dump

Farms and orchards

City greenways

City parks

The best place to start is close to home. If you have a property with trees, you may have some that need to be trimmed or removed over time. Ask neighbors and friends. Local tree services are constantly discarding raw wood and will be happy for you to take material off their hands. There are a variety of options. Explore your local area, find something that inspires you, and start asking around. You'll find that after the initial confusion, most people are quite receptive to the idea.

Unless the tree is on your own property, you'll need permission before you start hauling anything away. Strike up conversations with people about what you plan to do with the wood and show what you've already created. The concept of recycling wood waste into something beautiful strikes a chord with a lot of people, and you might find that the conversation inspires them to look differently at the trees around them. Or you might learn the stories of the wood you're sourcing. Getting permission is imperative, so take the time to do it right, even if you assume the wood is waste.

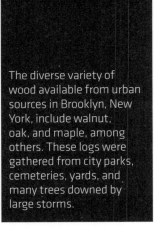
The diverse variety of wood available from urban sources in Brooklyn, New York, include walnut, oak, and maple, among others. These logs were gathered from city parks, cemeteries, yards, and many trees downed by large storms.

# IDENTIFYING TYPES OF WOOD

There are many varieties of trees in North America, but at your typical hardware store, your options are often limited to a handful of domestic hard- and softwoods. Your options expand somewhat in a hardwood supply store, but you can likely count the different types available on two hands. There's good reason for this, as the requirements for a species to be commercially viable are stringent. Consistent, sustainable supply, which can be provided in large enough quantities, is a must at the commercial level. At the same hardware store, you might count a couple dozen exotic species coming from overseas. It pains me to see this beautiful wood being shipped around the world when we have our own exotics all around us just waiting for a woodworker to dig into.

The woods available to you depend greatly on where you live. Living in the Southwest as I do, there are many native as well as imported trees. For example, in the Phoenix, Arizona, metro area alone there are eucalyptus, acacia, African sumac, olive, mesquite, palo verde, ironwood, pine, carob, elm, cottonwood, sissoo, and others—and this barely scratches the surface. Each species has multiple varieties with their own characteristics. And we can't forget to include all the different fruit and nut trees grown in backyards and orchards.

There are two basic classifications of wood: hardwood and softwood. This is a botanical distinction related to the structure of the fibers in the wood. Hardwoods (angiosperms) have vessels that carry water and form visible pores in the wood. Some examples of hardwoods are ash, beech, birch, mahogany, maple, oak, teak, and walnut.

Softwoods (gymnosperms) are typically evergreen (coniferous) trees that have no visible pores in the wood. Examples of softwoods are cedar, cypress, fir, pine, spruce, and redwood.

What does this mean for you and your project? Which wood is appropriate for building your project? Generally, hardwoods are indeed harder than softwoods, making softwoods somewhat easier to carve. There are notable exceptions to this rule (balsa, for example, is classified as a hardwood despite having softer wood).

Beyond that general classification, it would be difficult in the space we have here to classify the huge number of varieties available in urban and rural areas throughout the country. One of the distinct advantages of using found wood is that you greatly expand the varieties you have an opportunity to work with beyond what is commercially available.

Because of this, my advice is to learn what is available in your region and make use of what is abundant. You might learn that you don't enjoy working with every variety that you try, but you'll get to work with woods that most woodworkers never have the chance to work with, and there are many gems waiting to be found.

The immense variety can be overwhelming, so, short of taking an advanced botany class, the best way to begin understanding what trees are in your area is to go to a local tree nursery/garden center and explore, or talk to a local arborist and ask questions. There are print and online resources available, such as www.wood-database.com and regional field guides, that can help you identify wood. Step back and open your eyes to all the trees around. Soon enough, you will be a local expert as you begin to recognize the living forest that surrounds you. Before long, you'll be bugging your friends with endless tree trivia.

## IS THIS WOOD SUITABLE?

Just knowing what type of tree is in front of you is a good first step, but you still need to understand the wood inside that you'll be working with—not the bark and the leaves. Every species has its own characteristics, which come with benefits and challenges. I wouldn't spend too much time agonizing over whether to work with a certain variety of tree, however. Search any one of them and you will find that someone has probably cut it up and made something from it, so give it a shot. Knowing what to expect with less common varieties can only be learned from personal experience or talking to other local artisans who have already done it. Diving in like this makes the experience of cutting each log open that much more exciting, as you can't know exactly what you'll find.

## COMMON PROBLEMS AND DEFECTS

As you assess the specific log in front of you, there are defects to evaluate before deciding to work with it. As you will see later in this book, the problems that would normally make wood commercially unviable may be the mark that makes your work stand out. All the irregularities and discolorations that you find in a gnarly piece of wood add character and beauty, and they tell the tree's life story. Still, if you find a log that has degraded to the point of instability or is full of nails, you may want to skip it.

Sometimes, a log warps dramatically as soon as it is milled. Typically, this is because of tension or compression in the wood from stressors during growth. The result will be that as the wood is milled, the stresses that were evenly balanced become unbalanced, and the wood will move. With any wood that is cut up for lumber, some movement is unavoidable, but extreme movement ensures you'll have to start all over again with a new log.

As you begin to get your hands dirty and experience first-hand how to work with different types of trees and what oddities you can expect in the wood, you'll begin to understand when to work around an obstacle and when to scrap the wood. Any artisan will tell you the same—there's reading and understanding technically, and then there's doing. When you work with something like wood, something that was once a complex living organism, you must learn by doing. Besides, it's more fun that way.

## COMMON TIMBER ISSUES

**KNOTS**—These are formed when the tree grows around a dead branch. They add to the grain pattern, but the dead wood and bark of the branch can be loose, weak, or crumbly.

**PITCH**—This is the tarry sap found in pine trees. It can gum up tools and sandpaper.

**ROTTED WOOD (PUNKY)**—This wood is squishy, dry or wet, and it has no strength for milling.

**EMBEDDED FOREIGN OBJECTS**—Usually it's nails, screws, or wire fencing, all of which can damage milling equipment.

**COMPRESSION OR TENSION WOOD**—This is formed above and below branches, or in trees that lean or grow on steep hillsides. It causes excessive warpage after milling.

**INSECT DAMAGE**—These are holes and tunnels that can be attractive in finished pieces.

**FUNGUS AND MINERAL STAINS**—Fungus stains, or spalting, and streaks of mineral residue can be highly desirable features.

# GATHERING WOOD

**SAFETY TIP**
Remember, none of the logs you find will be worth getting a hernia over, so don't overextend yourself and always lift with your legs.

Once you find a log to mill, the feeling of anticipation as you dream of what you'll find inside and what you will make is exciting. Then reality hits, and you realize that logs are heavy and difficult to move. Before I ever worked up the courage to work with fallen trees, I would see one on the ground after a storm, get excited, and then give up because the thought of moving a large trunk was too intimidating. I'm a city boy. I don't have a truck or any heavy equipment to move a log, so I had to figure out what to do. You may find yourself in a similar situation, in which case you'll need to learn about the following:

Choosing manageable pieces to gather

Caring for the logs

Moving larger logs

A portable chainsaw mill, commonly known as an Alaskan mill

## SAFETY

Moving logs, even small ones, can be a dangerous activity. They are heavy, tend to roll, and are unwieldy. I asked my friend Todd Langford, a local sawyer who hauls logs daily, what his safety requirements are. He told me, "Your most important safety tools are patience and a little common sense. Even little logs can hurt you; trust me!" Beyond that, these are the safety tools he uses:

Emergency cell phone

Steel-toe boots

Eye protection

Gloves

Forearm guards

Hard hat

It's a good idea to have someone else with you for this activity, but if that's not possible, make sure you keep help a phone call away and keep that cell phone on your person. You would need help quickly if a log were to ever pin you down. Eye protection is also very important. You never want to take your eyes from a log that is still moving, but if something gets in your eye, it's tough to stay focused. Keep those eyes protected.

## CHOOSE MANAGEABLE PIECES

There is no shame in starting small. Some of the most satisfying woodworking projects can be made with smaller pieces of wood. Most projects in this book are created with raw wood sourced from logs no larger than 10 by 36 inches (25.5 by 91.5 cm). You'd be surprised by how heavy a green log even that small is. There's a lot you can learn from starting small that can be applied to the larger logs when you eventually move in that direction. You don't need any special tools to get started, just a strong pair of arms and a friend to help lift if it's too heavy. After a certain point, a log is just too big to lift by hand.

## CARING FOR THE LOGS

When you find a fresh log, paint the ends with two to three coats of latex paint. This will slow the moisture evaporation out of the exposed log ends, which should minimize cracking. You can skip this step if the log has already been sitting for a long period, as coating the end will no longer help seal in moisture.

There is some disagreement over how long you can let a log lie before cutting it up, and the answer depends on whether it can be kept in an environment that will preserve the wood inside. In the arid southwest, I often let logs season for a time before cutting into them. Wood becomes much harder and tougher once it has dried, which makes cutting more difficult. On the other hand, a partially dried log can be less prone to some of the more extreme drying problems described in more detail on page 57.

## PORTABLE MILLS

When you come upon a log that requires a trailer, winches, and other equipment to load and haul, consider milling the log into lumber on-site. Chainsaw mills were invented for this purpose (and are discussed in greater detail on page 46). One option is to work with a sawyer who has a portable sawmill. There are many of these mills out there, and for those heavy and cumbersome logs, it is a great solution. Hauling away slabs of lumber and cleaning up leftover sawdust is much easier than moving a three-thousand-pound (1,361 kg) green log.

## MOVING LARGER LOGS

I'm going to be honest with you: Personally, I don't attempt moving larger logs without professional help. Picking up the phone and calling someone with the experience and equipment is often the wisest thing to do, especially when starting out. You can join in the work and try to learn as much as you can before attempting on your own. Great sawyers like Todd with years of experience are a wonderful resource, so ask plenty of questions.

Urban logs waiting to be milled

Tools of the log moving trade

### STEP 1

### ASSESSING THE LOG AND SURROUNDINGS

Before you move the log, take a good look at it and the environment around it. Is it in a neighbor's yard? How far is it from vehicle access? Are there foreign objects embedded in the wood? Every situation is different. Only after this assessment should you decide if the tree is worth extracting and how. Make sure the trunk is as straight and round as possible by trimming any major protrusions with a chainsaw. If there are lots of branches coming out of the log, it probably came from higher up in the tree, is less likely to be milled into usable lumber, and may make it more suitable for firewood. Keep that in mind before you decide to haul it away.

As a rule, it's best to leave the surroundings in as good a shape as you found them, especially if it's a residential or commercial area. Look for sprinkler heads, landscaping, and edges of buildings and figure out how to avoid damaging them. What seemed to a neighbor to be a nice favor can quickly turn into a major inconvenience for them. Remember this and be considerate.

### STEP 2

### TURNING, ROLLING, AND LIFTING

To manipulate a large log, you will need a cant hook, which is essentially a large lever used for rolling logs. The hook needs to be the appropriate size for the log you are working with or else it won't get a proper grip and will make moving the log more dangerous. The proper way to use a cant hook is to first make sure the hook has grabbed into the wood, not just the bark, and maintain the proper form throughout the turn. Never pull a log toward yourself with the hook. Start low and lift with your legs pushing the log away from your body. Don't extend your arms higher than your shoulders. Using the cant hook, you can roll extremely heavy logs, which will make you feel very strong. If you aren't careful, the log will quickly teach you that it is bigger than you are and very dangerous. Be mindful of the rollback after you have moved a log. When you let go of the cant hook the trunk can shift, sending the hook flying back in your general direction and potentially pinning your feet or legs to the ground if you are in the path of danger.

To turn a log, you can place a wedge on one end of the log and use a cant hook on the other end. The ramp will inhibit forward progress on one end, acting as the fulcrum, while on the far end, as you turn with your cant hook, the log will slowly but surely rotate in the direction you desire.

## HAULING TOOLS

Cant hook
Steel digging bar
Hookaroon
Electric winch or come-along
Logging chain (x2)
3/4" (19 mm) rope
20" (51 cm) chainsaw
Hi-lift farmer's jack
Large wedges
A few 2×10-inch (5 × 25.5 cm) boards
Optional Items:
Skidding plate
Metal detector
Boulder moving dolly
Logging arch
Tractor
Trailer mounted crane
Forklift

## STEP 3

### SKIDDING

The term skidding here is used loosely to cover the various methods of getting the log from where it fell to the trailer that will be used to haul it away. Ideally, you could get the trailer close enough so that all you need to do is roll the log up to it with your cant hook. You must be quite close, however, because this method quickly becomes backbreaking work.

Alternatively, skidding the logs along the ground is a viable way to move logs over a distance. Attach one end of the log to a winch on your trailer, or ideally, a tractor, by way of a skidding hook or skidding chain, and lift the end of the log. The next step is just causing forward progress with the tractor or winch, letting one end drag on the ground. The key is getting one end up or on a skidding plate; otherwise, it will take a tremendous amount of force to pull the log as it digs into the ground. There will be a trench of dirt and destroyed grass in the log's wake using this method, so if you are in a landscaped area, lay a path of plywood to protect from any damage.

A great tool for hauling is a logging arch. This tool allows for the log to be balanced between two wheels and has a long handle to give plenty of leverage. The tires greatly reduce the damage to the surroundings. Hauling this logging arch by hand for any distance is a strenuous task, but if you have a tractor, all-terrain vehicle (ATV), or muck truck available, you have some useful options for hauling.

A log hanging on a logging arch. Capable of moving incredibly heavy logs, it's best in the hands of a professional.

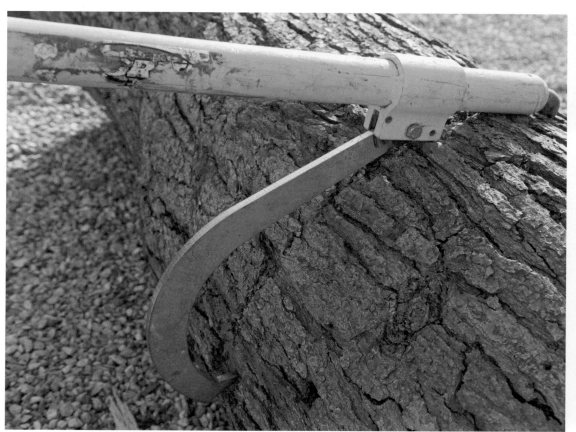

A cant hook bites into a large log.

## STEP 4

## LOADING

Getting the log loaded from the ground onto the trailer is one of the trickiest steps. If you can load your trailer from the side, a loading ramp works great. Loading ramps are essentially ramps with a series of vertical cauls that act as stops, so the log can be rolled step-by-step up the ramp without the log rolling back to the bottom with each roll. Any time you load from the side, your trailer must be properly supported, as they are not built to take pressure in that direction and can easily tip unless outfitted with outriggers or other methods of support.

A winch or come-along can be used to load from the back of a trailer. Make sure you wedge the back of the trailer

with a block of wood to keep it stable during the loading process. If possible, your winch rope should run through a pulley positioned several feet (around 1 or 2 m) above the rear of the trailer by way of metal arch. The ideal trailer for hauling is very sturdy and has some modifications made for loading and unloading heavy logs.

Sawyer Todd Langford rolls a log with a cant hook.

## UNLOADING

Loading the log is only one half of the equation. The second half is unloading the log. Safety is key, since the forces of gravity can cause logs to move downward in an uncontrolled manner. Any person who has unloaded logs from a trailer understands that heavy equipment is very helpful here. Operators at small mills around the country all rave about the advantages of having a forklift or grapple loader.

If you're able to tilt the bed of the trailer, dumping the log and driving away is one way to unload, or reversing the winching technique talked about in the loading step can work. A professional will have the tools required to load and unload large logs, which is one of the primary reasons I like to rely on their help. If you find yourself moving lots of logs, you will begin collecting your own set of tools suited to the task, with your specific set of circumstances in mind. If you are like me and don't collect logs daily, seek help. Once your first large log has been successfully collected, you will breathe a sigh of relief. You can begin the next and more rewarding step: milling.

Preparing to skid a log using a chain and winch

Todd's custom logging arch and mini tractor setup

Chains used for hauling logs

A well-loved forklift

Hook used for hauling logs

# PART TWO
# MILLING AND SEASONING

When you think about milling lumber, images of massive saws, heavy trucks, and industrial-scale tools may be the first that come to mind. Even local operations milling urban and reclaimed trees have tools outside the access of the typical hobbyist. As a hobbyist, what is the best way to approach this activity that is normally reserved to the industrial process? The answer is simple: think smaller and lower volume. You'll be amazed what you can accomplish with a few key skills and tools. The tools you already have access to aren't that different from their industrial cousins, just smaller and lighter duty. We'll be dealing with band-saws, circular saws, and chainsaws, so it's just a matter of taking the tools we have and making them work.

As a hobbyist sawyer, you've also unlocked a whole new source of wood. All around you there are trees that need to trimmed—trees with limbs that come down in big storms or are at the end of their life. Properly milled, these trees are a diverse and figured palette that are difficult to find at your local woodworking store. The neighborhood, city, or landscape around you is full of wood that someone is treating as trash. At best, it's being turned into mulch or firewood, but it begs to be more. What could mean more than a dinner table made from a tree that stood in your grandfather's yard? Imagine the amazing story you'll have to tell every time you use your serving tray made from a log you gathered down the street from your house? We'll talk more about this in the section on finding raw logs, but once you're able to process a log into usable boards, you've expanded the horizons of the types of wood you have access to.

As an enthusiast, you don't need to be able to mill ten logs quickly. You can take time to assess each log and apply your craft to maximize its potential. This is a big difference between commercial and hobbyist approaches to milling and is an advantage to you as a hobbyist. Taking your time with the process shouldn't be a problem, as it's supposed to be enjoyable. After all, this is a labor of love. In this section, you'll learn a few approaches, each applicable in different situations, depending on the size of log you're staring down.

These are the three basic approaches that I'll talk about:

Milling in your workshop with a bandsaw

Milling in your backyard with a chainsaw mill

Working with a professional sawyer

# WORKSHOP MILLING

I grew up near an apple tree; I frequently played under its branches and enjoyed its fruit. The memories from each summer as apples ripened are still as vivid as ever. Every summer, my siblings and I harvested and processed the apples for use in pies, apple crisps, and dried apple snacks. We all complained loudly about having to work in the heat of summer, but this hasn't soured my memory of that apple tree. It also has history for my co-author David. Several years ago, when the tree was in full bloom, he married my sister under that tree. I walked her down the aisle and stood in the wedding. It was a solid presence in our lives from childhood to adulthood. The log we cut from this tree has special meaning to me: We had some pretty rocky times growing up, but the memory of this tree is a reminder of goodness in the hard times and the light after.

A couple of years ago, after the tree became diseased and died, my mom decided to part ways with the property, and all that is left is this log. In a very real sense, this log connects me with my childhood and a time that is no more, so I hope to memorialize this memory by making good use of the wood and creating something meaningful.

If you are anything like me, you are inspired by seeing something made from a huge slab of wood taken from a very large log. Something about the scale resonates with most people. Much of the time, however, you will be limited to milling smaller pieces. This has several advantages. A professional mill would not touch a log like this. It is too small and riddled with holes from beetles, carpenter bees, and termites. The imperfections, though commercially unviable, make it desirable to a hobbyist who may have a connection with the tree or just love its unique character.

Small logs are easier to get a hold of, move, and mill, and you can make a lot out of smaller pieces of wood, as you'll see later in this book. What better way to get your arms around the process than starting small? The wood is just as beautiful inside, and you'll find yourself paying more attention to the finer details.

A log under two feet (61 cm) long and a foot (30.5 cm) across is a perfect example for an introductory milling project. Whether you are trimming limbs from a large tree or using the trunk section from a smaller tree, these sorts of logs are abundant even if you're in a city. Before splitting, most firewood comes from these sorts of log. There are likely a wide variety of species available, some unique to the area you live. You should have no trouble finding something similar to begin milling.

Bandsaws are a very common workshop tool. They come in a variety of sizes, but for this purpose, the smallest size you'll want to use is one with a six-inch (15 cm) clearance for cutting height. Typically, this equates to what they call a 14-inch (35.5 cm) bandsaw and is the most commonly found size in a small hobbyist home workshop. Besides the saw you are going to use, the biggest consideration for milling small logs is to keep the log from shifting during the cut, which is why you will be making a bandsaw sled.

A bandsaw sled can be included in the broad category of woodworking jigs, which is a purpose-built tool made by a craftsman to help with a specific task. There are a million different jigs you can build and a million ways to build them.

Urban mesquite slabs (or slices of a log) stacked with stickers (thin pieces of wood used as spacers for drying)

Note that Silas is wearing safety glasses, hearing protection, and a breathing mask.

## STEP 1

## PREPARING YOUR BANDSAW SLED

A bandsaw sled is simple really—it's just a flat piece of plywood that the log rides on while the first cuts are made. The plywood should have a way of securing the log against shifting side to side or rolling. Keeping it steady is crucial. When working with a whole log, the blade will want to roll the log down in the direction it is spinning on the first few cuts since the log is round and the outside edge has no support directly under it. The sled will counteract this and keep things rolling smoothly.

To build a basic sled, take that $1/2$-inch (13 mm) plywood and cut a section about a foot (30.5 cm) wide and between 2 and 3 feet (0.5 to 1 m) long depending on the length of logs you are milling. This piece of plywood should be rectangular. Make at least three right angle supports, again using the same $1/2$-inch (13 mm) plywood. These will be screwed into the log near either end and in the middle. The perpendicular surface of the support will be screwed to the sled. It's a simple jig to make but makes a big impact, just as any good jig should.

To keep the cut straight, the sled will either need to ride in the miter slot (a groove on the bandsaw table that is parallel with the blade) or ride against the fence (an adjustable guide that sits on top of the bandsaw table). Either way, you will need to make sure that your blade is adjusted parallel with the guide of your choice.

A simple but effective bandsaw sled made from $1/2$-inch (13 mm) plywood and wood screws

## CORE SKILLS

Splitting and trimming a log to fit to your saw

Supporting a log for stability

Making a straight cut in a log with a bandsaw

Slabbing lumber

## MATERIALS

Small log

1/2" (13 mm) plywood

Wood screws

## TOOLS

Bandsaw (at least a 14" [35.5 cm] bandsaw with 6" [15 cm] clearance)

Resaw blade for bandsaw (at least 3/4" [19 mm] wide, 2–3 teeth per inch [2.5 cm])

Bandsaw sled (you'll make)

1–2 roller support stands

Splitting wedges and small sledgehammer

Screwdriver

Drawknife (optional)

Screwing the log support into the sled

Attaching the log to the supports

A nice straight first cut using the bandsaw sled. Notice the roller stand supporting the back of the sled.

## PREPARING THE LOG FOR THE BANDSAW

Even with a small log, a 6-inch (15 cm) limit is pretty, well, limiting. When using a bandsaw sled, you lose at least a half inch (13 mm) of capacity, so now you're looking at a capacity in the range of 5 1/2 inches (14 cm), which is likely too small to accommodate your chosen log. How can we overcome this? One way is to break the log into smaller pieces manually before milling. Since small logs like this are essentially firewood sized, they are simple to split using a couple splitting wedges and small sledgehammer (see sidebar). I like this method because you can more accurately control where the log is going to split. If you want to keep the center intact, you can split off the outside edges, selectively choosing which parts to keep pristine for milling.

There are bandsaws that offer more than 6 inches (15 cm) of capacity as well as modifications that can be added onto bandsaws to give them more capacity, so if breaking the log up doesn't sound like your style, consider modifying your bandsaw or getting access to one with a bigger capacity. Regardless, the process is the same for any bandsaw.

It is a good idea to remove the roughest of the bark from the wood as there are often bits of sand and dirt that have accumulated inside. These are hard on saw blades, causing them to dull more quickly. The best tool for this job is a drawknife. If the wood has been sitting for some time, the bark is much more likely to fall off with minimal assistance. Also, logs are frequently not straight and have odd protrusions that will interfere with placing on the bandsaw sled, so you may also need to trim some sections off with a small chainsaw.

Driving the wedge into the end of the log to begin the split

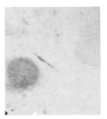

Expanding the split with a second wedge

The apple log after a successful split

Splitting a log with twisted grain. Notice the tendency for the split to turn away from the wedge.

Trimming a small log with a small electric chainsaw

Using a drawknife to remove bark

## SPLITTING WOOD BY HAND

Riving is the age-old technique for splitting logs to size. There are woodworkers who use this method almost exclusively for roughly shaping all their boards. For riving, you must use the highest quality logs with straight, even grain; you should also use green wood to ease the splitting process. Here, we use wedges and a sledge hammer, but a tool called a froe is the best for the job.

Mark approximately where you want the split to be on the end of the log and on the side. Next, drive one of the wedges in just a bit where you marked on the end of the log until you see a small split form. When you see this split, go to the side of the log and about 6 inches (15 cm) to a foot (30.5 cm) down your mark, drive that wedge in until it stays in on its own. Alternate driving the end wedge and the side wedge. When you see the split reaching close to the side wedge, remove it and drive it in again another 6 to 12 inches (15 to 30.5 cm) down your mark again. If you have a third wedge, you don't have to remove the first side wedge. After the third wedge is in, the course will likely be pretty much set, so focus a bit more on the wedge on the end and help complete the split with those side wedges.

The smaller the log, the less time this process will take. You may find if you have a log with lots of twisting grain that splitting straight is not possible. Do your best. This method of splitting is also possible with very large and long logs, so if you have a longer log you wish to mill on your bandsaw but need to break down first, this is a viable method.

## MAKING THE FIRST CUT

Secure the log (or log piece) to the sled using wood screws. Adjust the bandsaw fence so that the sled just fits between it and the blade, making the edge of the sled an approximate reference for where the cut will be made. The log should hang over that line enough for the first cut to be made along the entire length of the log. Before actually setting the loaded sled on the bandsaw, evaluate the weight and length of the log. If the log is too heavy, you will need to support it on both the front and back of the bandsaw table so you don't overstress the support structure of the bandsaw. Before you start the first cut, double check that your bandsaw table is adjusted square with the blade.

The longer the log, the trickier maneuvering the log will be, so don't be afraid to ask for a second set of hands to help steady the log. Keep the sled going nice and straight, not allowing it to swing away from the fence for any reason. Doing so would put a lot of stress on the thin bandsaw blade. Make your cut at a rather slow pace. When you are going at the right pace, you can hear your bandsaw sing. If the singing becomes a scream or slows down to a whine, you know you need to back off. If you smell something like a campfire, you're either going too slowly or you aren't cutting in a straight line, and your blade is under stress, causing the blade to heat up.

Silas adjusting the bandsaw before milling

Start of the first cut of an apple tree limb

Milling without the sled. Notice the two flat sides achieved with the first two cuts.

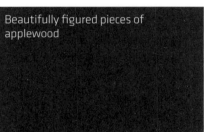

Beautifully figured pieces of applewood

This applewood will make an appearance in a later project.

## STEP 4

## SLAB THE LOG

Once you have made the first cut, turn the log flat side down in the sled and repeat the process. This next cut gives you two flat sides square with each other. At this point, you can choose to take the log off the sled and run it directly against the fence. I find that removing the sled is easier to manage at this point. Once the reference faces are cut, sequentially cut the log up into slices, more frequently referred to as slabs.

## STEP 5

## STACK THE SLABS FOR SEASONING

As you cut slices off your log, you should be stacking the pieces up with small stickers. These are thin pieces of wood that act as spacers, providing airflow to the green wood for proper drying. This is covered more in the section on seasoning your wood, but just make sure put one of these stickers every 12 inches (30.5 cm) or so for a small log like this. Build the stack to the side where it won't interfere with your work. The process of seasoning wood is covered in depth on page 57.

Once you are done, you should be looking at a small stack of rough boards. You'll need to dry and flatten the boards before using them, but it is a satisfying feeling to have made boards, even if small, from a raw log.

# BACKYARD MILLING

You may at some point decide to move beyond the size constraints of a shop bandsaw. As much as you can do with smaller pieces of wood, the allure of working with a larger slab of wood is hard to resist—and you should feel empowered to do so. The tools are readily available for milling large slabs of wood in your backyard or wherever your log happens to be. The tool of choice is called a chainsaw mill, which consists of a chainsaw outfitted with a special milling attachment. These attachments are available from a variety of manufacturers and were developed specifically for portability, allowing foresters and loggers to bring the mill to logs that couldn't easily be hauled intact. They are simple devices for the most part, equipping standard chainsaws with an adjustable support system parallel to the blade. This allows for a straight and accurate cut.

Most homeowner chainsaws have 16 to 20 inch (40.5 to 51 cm) bars. While it may be possible to use an electric chainsaw for very small logs, this task is better suited to a powerful gas-powered saw equipped with a sharp chain. Not all chainsaws are created equally, and you may find that not all are up to the task. A good rule of thumb would be to select brands that arborists rely on. Lesser saws will end up costing you more in time, money, and frustration later. In addition to the selection of the saw is the matter of the chain, which is what does the actual cutting. A sharp chain is critical and a ripping chain is specially designed for efficiently cutting lengthwise down a log. Without this, you'll find yourself cutting for much longer, putting more wear on the saw, wasting more wood, and tiring yourself in the process.

Sawyer Ty Moser explains chainsaw milling to Silas.

| CORE SKILLS | MATERIALS | TOOLS | SAFETY |
|---|---|---|---|
| Milling medium to large logs into slabs | Log | Gas chainsaw | Gloves |
| | | Ripping chain | Ear protection |
| | | Sharpening file | Facemask |
| | | Chainsaw mill attachment | Chaps |
| | | Log support | Milling assistant |
| | | Extension ladder | Steel-toed boots |
| | | Wedges | |
| | | 1/4" (6.5 mm) lag bolts and ratchet | |
| | | 3/4" (19 mm) stickers | |
| | | Spacer blocks (optional) | |

Silas and Ty. More about Ty at www.monolocoworkshop.com.

Mesquite log awaits the chainsaw mill.

By the time you purchase a milling attachment, worthy chainsaw, ripping chains, and accessories, you'll have spent several thousand dollars. This is a significant cost for most people, especially for a casual hobbyist. This is a good excuse to find a like-minded person who has the gear you need, so I suggest that you make some friends and pitch your resources together. Better to owe them a few beers and share equipment than to drain your savings on tools you may rarely use.

A note about backyard milling: You must be willing and ready to improvise and adjust on the go. Even for experienced hands, the challenge every log brings is slightly different. As soon as you step out into the real world, you will find obstacles that need figuring out, so be as prepared as you can, think creatively, and never try something your gut tells you isn't safe. (If your gut doesn't have a good safety record, this may not be the hobby for you.)

Chainsaws are powerful, and when used improperly, dangerous tools. All safety instructions contained in the user's manual for both the saw and milling attachment should be observed when milling. You should be well familiar with the proper operation of your saw and attachment before beginning this process. Also, wearing the appropriate safety gear is crucial. At a minimum, gloves, ear protection, facemask, chaps, and steel-toed boots should be worn, as well as having the help of a similarly equipped assistant to safely move and operate the saw with milling attachment.

## STEP 1

### PREPARE THE CHAINSAW

Milling is not a light-duty task for any chainsaw. Your saw should be tuned up and able to run flat out for a significant period. This is where lesser saws will quickly make their inferior engineering known. The chain should be sharpened, and you should be prepared to sharpen mid-process at some point as well. Tension on the chain should be snug. Once the saw is filled with gas and oil, go ahead and affix the milling attachment.

Securing the ladder used for the first pass

## STEP 2

### STABILIZE THE LOG

A log must be well secured before beginning the cut to avoid shifting, which will cause a potentially unsafe situation as well as spoiling the board. For large logs, this isn't typically an issue. Prevent rolling using wedges, which can be made from stumps or tree limbs. When it comes to using a powerful tool such as a chainsaw, you need to be able to focus, so eliminating elements of surprise is key.

## STEP 3

## SECURE THE LADDER FOR THE FIRST CUT

With the log secured, it is almost time for the cutting to begin. Logs come in any variation of size and shapes, so there is no reference for a straight cut, but for the chainsaw to be at all useful, you need a flat and straight surface for a guide. A common technique is to use a ladder affixed to the top of the log using 1/4-inch (6.5 mm) lag bolts fastened directly into the wood. The first time you do this, you'll need to drill holes in the rungs of the ladder. Position the ladder so that it hugs the log as securely as possible and sits level. Drill pilot holes before driving the bolts in. Purpose-built chainsaw mill guides are also available.

Cutting the first pass with a ladder

Setting the mill's cut depth with premade spacers

## STEP 4

## MAKE THE FIRST CUT

The first cut is the trickiest, mostly due to needing to affix the ladder. The other unique aspect to this step is that you'll need to adjust the mill attachment to account for the thickness of the ladder, so the opening between the guide bar and the chainsaw bar will be wide. Also, make sure you also consider the depth you drove the lag bolts into the log so that your cut is well clear of any metal.

A great little tip I got from my friend Ty for setting the depth consistently is to make two sets of precut spacer blocks. Each set should have a couple 1-inch (25 mm) spacer blocks, a 1/2-inch (13 mm) block, and a 1/4-inch (6.5 mm) block. Make sure they are accurate and consistent.

Before you and your assistant guide the mill onto the ladder, start the chainsaw up and make sure it is warmed up enough. When starting a cut, get the saw up to full speed and ease the saw into the wood. Don't force it and be aware of the tendency for the saw to shift a bit when first biting into the wood and starting the cutting track. As the cut progresses, keep the saw running full stop, keeping constant light contact with the wood just enough for the chain to continually bite. Your assistant will be on the far side of the blade, helping to keep the mill perpendicular to the log.

You'll get a feel for your saw as you go and how to react to keep everything going at maximum efficiency. The tone of the saw will tell you a lot. The sound and vibration when it's running full out with little to no resistance means you can increase the pace ever so slightly. When you sense that the chain is still moving at or near full speed, but the saw is having to work harder for it, keep it steady and don't push further. The next sound you'll hear is the engine bogging down. You'll feel the chain slow down noticeably. It's tempting to try forcing the cut at this point, but remember that the chain is doing the cutting, not the power of your pushing. By letting the chain move at full speed, you will get the most cutting power.

Once the saw is well on its way, you or your assistant should drive a wedge at the end of the log to keep the saw blade from getting pinched. If it's a long log, you'll need to continue this process occasionally as you move down the cut. If the blade becomes bound between the log and the slab above, you'll come to a quick standstill.

Peeling back that first rough layer of the log

Getting an initial taste of the character that was locked inside the log is always exciting.

Using a wedge at the back of a cut to prevent blade pinching

## STEP 5
### SLAB THE LOG

Barring complication, the next cuts should be easier and quicker. Remove the ladder, reset the milling attachment to cut the thickness of slab desired, and slice the log. Chainsaws have a fairly rough cutting pattern, so be sure to leave at least 1/2 inch (13 mm) extra thickness from your final intended slab thickness to allow for planing.

At this point, if you can, prop one end of the log up on a notched stump to introduce a slope, so you can use gravity in the cutting process. Make sure that the log is secure against rolling or shifting.

Starting each cut is the hardest part of this process. With no ladder to rely on, you'll have to use only the front guide bar at first. Make sure you keep the lateral supports centered on the log during this part, to keep the chainsaw bar from dipping. Once you are in as far as the back guide bar, you can allow the saw to move right up to hug the log and ride along the skid.

Starting a cut. Note the lateral support bar positioned over the log.

## STEP 6
### STACK THE SLABS

The process of drying begins immediately upon being cut, and depending on the weather, can be quite rapid. It is important to start stacking slabs right away. Find a place out of the way of milling operations. Starting with the second slab, stack each consecutively with 3/4-inch (19 mm) thick spacers called stickers every 18 inches (45.5 cm) placed between the boards. These will promote even air flow. It's also a good idea to label the boards now with a grease pencil or by stapling paper tags to the ends to keep track of where they came from in the log to refer to later when beginning to build projects.

There are two things that never seem to fail with these projects. One is the satisfied feeling when the job is done. Second is that it always takes longer than you initially plan. Something inevitably comes up during the process to slow things down, but in the end, the feeling of satisfaction wins out over any frustrations.

Stacked mesquite with stickers

Silas and Ty take a pass with the chainsaw. Note that the chainsaw is perpendicular to the log.

# USING A SAWYER

## WHAT IS THE LIVE EDGE?

The live edge is the term used to describe the side or sides of a board that include the outer edge of the tree, reminding us of the board's origins from the live tree.

While traveling the country and documenting for *Felled*, Silas and I heard one thing over and over; when people were just starting to get into woodworking, they underestimated just how heavy and unwieldy wood can be. You may come across a beautiful piece of a trunk of a large tree and have dreams about everything you could create from it. But that piece of wood is never going to fit in a pickup truck. You're never going to be able to find a band saw big enough to mill it. You've entered a whole new world, and it's time to make friends with a local sawyer.

The bandsaw mill at Wine Glass Bar Saw Mill in Phoenix, Arizona, cuts into an Aleppo pine log.

David watches as sawyer Rex Condie loads an Aleppo pine log on the bandsaw mill.

## STEP 1

### SEEK OUT A SAWYER

A sawyer is someone who operates a sawmill and, believe it or not, there's one near you. When we first learned that there was a busy sawmill right along the fence of our local international airport, we figured it was a joke. If central Phoenix, Arizona, has a great urban sawmill, I'd bet your city does as well. Start by talking to a local arborist who removes trees or search online for a sawyer. Visiting a small local mill can be a great way to begin the conversation about getting usable boards out of a large piece of wood.

## STEP 2

### DECIDE HOW TO MILL YOUR LOG

For most milling and kiln drying (more on that later), we turn to our good friends at Wine Glass Bar Saw Mill. We arranged with them to have the log picked up and transferred to their yard. You'll need to decide what sort of lumber you want out of your log. If you're starting with a 36-inch (91.5 cm) tree trunk, you'll need to consider the maximum width the mill can accept as well as what needs to be trimmed to create a cant. A cant is a log with at least one flat side. To safely mill a round log, it must sit securely on the mill track, pressed firmly against the metal uprights that extend above the mill's bed. Often, this requires trimming one or more sides flat with the saw, creating a cant. It's quite likely that your 36-inch (91.5 cm) trunk will yield slabs that are approximately 32 inches (81 cm) wide or even less without a live edge.

An Aleppo pine log is loaded onto the bandsaw mill.

Once the log is safely on the bandsaw mill, the saw will pass through the cant to create slabs. Depending on the type of wood and how you'll dry it, you'll want to think about how thick to slice each slab. If the wood is prone to twisting and you don't have access to a kiln, then you may want to take 2-inch (5 cm) or even 3-inch (7.5 cm) passes. These will give you plenty of room to later level, plane, and sand the slabs down to a 1 1/2- or 2-inch (4 or 5 cm) usable board. The most common way to mill a log is a flat or plain sawn pattern. This makes horizontal slices through the entire log and produces the most lumber from a log. Another less common method of milling is a pattern called quarter sawn, resulting in smaller boards with a beautiful wood grain. Talk with your sawyer about the best method for your project.

### WHAT IS A QUARTER SAWN PATTERN?

Quarter sawn logs are first cut lengthwise into quarters and then each quarter is turned 45 degrees and sawed in slices, perpendicular to the growth rings of the tree. This process results in a different wood grain pattern than is typical for a flat sawn board. In some species, like oak, there are features that can only be seen when the wood is cut this way. Quarter sawn wood results in a narrower board, but the visible grain pattern can be stunning.

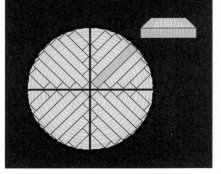

Wine Glass Bar Saw Mill is located just outside the fence of a large international airport.

A freshly resawn black acacia slab

Tim Adams removes a nail from a log. Nails are a major problem with urban logs. They can cause major damage to a saw blade.

## MILL

The sawyer will take extra care to look out for metal that can ruin his mill's blade. Many sawyers will manually push the saw through the wood to feel any problem that may arise with each cut. Milling is a delicate operation, and a good sawyer will know just how their mill should sound and feel. As you pull each slab off, inspect them and decide if you need to make any thickness adjustments for the next pass. Don't be afraid to ask to stop cutting for a minute and use water to wash away all the sawdust and bring out the grain to see what you're getting. Rex always says that cutting into a log is like Christmas morning, opening a present and seeing what beauty was locked away inside.

David watches as Rex and Tim resaw a black acacia slab that will be used for the dining table project on page 116.

## STACK AND PREPARE FOR DRYING

Once the log is milled, stack the slabs with stickers separating them. Find a level spot and lay down stickers (you can use thin boards) every few feet down the length of your slab. Then place a slab on top and line up a new set of stickers above the first row. Continue until the whole log is stacked back in order with the stickers between. At this point, you'll need to have a plan for drying the wood. We talk about your options in the Seasoning Lumber section on page 56.

You've finished a big part of the process. We always love spending an early morning at the mill unlocking the potential of a discarded urban tree. But this is just the beginning of the story. The drying process can be unpredictable and will largely determine what you're able to make with a large log.

David stands next to one of the bookmatched black acacia slabs that will form the top of a dinner table. A bookmatch is when two adjacent slabs taken from the same log are opened like the pages of a book, creating a mirror image of the grain pattern. This tree came from a neighborhood in Phoenix, Arizona, and was diverted from a landfill by the tree service that removed it.

Various wood is stacked with stickers in a kiln for drying.

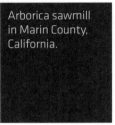

Arborica sawmill in Marin County, California.

# SEASONING LUMBER

I remember the success I felt after having finally obtaining a fallen tree, hauling it, and milling it into beautiful two-by-eight foot (0.5 by 2.5 m) slabs. As I moved from the familiar world of saws and mechanical processes to the unknown world of seasoning lumber, the suspense grew. After several months had passed and the drying process was complete, the material was still beautiful, but my pristine slabs had significantly warped and now contained numerous cracks. This describes my introduction to the world of drying lumber, the story told in *Felled*. Likely, you will experience some of these same feelings and obstacles.

When talking to sawyers all over the country, we learned that the hardest part of the raw lumber process is properly seasoning the material. The difficulty is that it feels much more like a science experiment than woodworking. You can't force it into submission. There is no rushing it, and no matter how hard you try, the wood will do what it wants and not necessarily the way you want. What may have started out as beautiful slabs of building material may end up so warped and cracked as to become unrecognizable. Are you scared yet? Well, fear not. Though the process can be somewhat unpredictable, you can minimize any problems with simple considerations and end up with some great material to use for your projects.

## SEASONING VERSUS DRYING

You'll notice we use the term seasoning lumber for the process of drying wood. The first time I heard this term used was when I was in Marin County, California, north of San Francisco, visiting a salvage milling operation nestled in the hills next to an idyllic creamery. The sawyer, Evan Shively, showed me a massive barn full of stack upon stack of lumber slabs, many of which had been sitting for up to a decade. He described a process akin to the art of storing and aging fine wine—following the natural timeline with fastidious care toward each piece and accounting for each species' unique tendencies, learned over years of careful observation. The results were pristine and highly sought after by world-class craftsman for use in breathtaking pieces. It's not just about getting the wood dry; there's another almost intangible element of quality that can only come with time and attention. Recognizing that there's more at play than just the wood being dry, we use the term seasoning. With that in mind, in this section, we will cover the following:

Principles of seasoning lumber

Methods of seasoning lumber

Steps for seasoning your lumber at home

## MEASURING WOOD MOISTURE CONTENT

Moisture content of wood is determined by comparing the weight of the water contained to the weight of the wood with all the moisture removed. To determine the moisture content in any given piece of wood, the simple formula Moisture Content Percent = (Water Weight / Dry Wood Weight) x 100 is used. For instance, let's say I have a green piece of lumber that weighs 10 pounds (4.5 kg); I put it in the oven until every bit of moisture has escaped and then weigh it again, and now it weighs 4 pounds (2 kg). The 6 pounds (3 kg) of water escaped divided by the 4 pounds of remaining wood equals 1.5. Converting that to a percentage equals 150 percent moisture content. This is the most accurate way of measuring moisture content, but difficult, so most people use a moisture meter, which measures the electrical resistance of the wood and calculates the moisture content instantly.

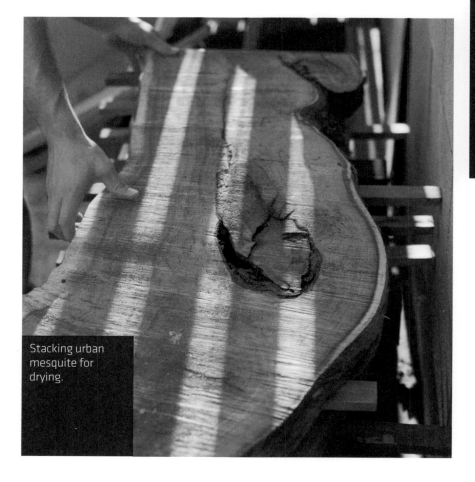

Stacking urban mesquite for drying.

# PRINCIPLES OF SEASONING LUMBER

When a tree is alive, it is full of water, just like every other life form. As soon as it dies, the drying process begins, and the wood will eventually reach equilibrium with its surroundings, whether it takes one year or twenty. Drying is determined by three basic factors: ambient air moisture, air flow, and temperature. As the wood dries, it changes in shape and size. Imagine watching a time-lapse of a flower drying out—the petals shrivel and change their shape and position. Wood is no different. The more gently moisture can be removed from the wood, the fewer defects will occur, as the stresses are very gradually introduced and the wood has time to equalize pressure evenly throughout the board.

The time right after the wood is milled and the moisture is at its peak is when it's most susceptible to forming these defects. There are two classifications of moisture in wood: free water and bound water. Free water is just as it sounds: water that is surrounding the cells of the wood grain and not contained by any structure. Early in the drying process, this type of moisture quickly escapes, leaving behind the bound water contained within the cell walls of the wood itself. This process can happen violently, leaving the wood checked and warped, so this early stage of the drying is key.

Next comes the stage that requires much more patience; removing the bound moisture. This moisture must work much harder to escape, but

Stacking wood for seasoning

eventually it will, reaching equilibrium with the atmosphere around it. The thicker the lumber has been milled, the lengthier the seasoning process. A common estimate is one year of drying time for each inch (2.5 cm) of thickness. Much depends on the climate in your region. In Phoenix, Arizona, for instance, our summer temperatures are commonly over 100°F (38°C), with humidity levels under 10 percent. Those two factors will greatly shorten drying speed, meaning a one inch (2.5 cm) slab can dry in a matter of weeks. The target moisture content for furniture-grade lumber is typically in the 6 to 12 percent range, though the best range for you depends on your climate. The more humid your climate, the higher in that range your lumber can be.

Remember the term seasoning? Just because a board has reached the target moisture content doesn't mean the seasoning process has completed. There are real differences between a slab of wood that has been air-drying for ten years and one that's just barely reached the target moisture content. A well-seasoned slab has been dry for a long time and has had a chance to gently adjust to many seasons of weather. During this time, the wood mellows out, and any lingering tensions are eased away as much as possible. Waiting for the full seasoning process isn't always possible, but if you can, give the boards as much time as you can to season.

# SEASONING METHODS

Kiln drying is an option for seasoning lumber more quickly. It applies all the same principles as air drying, but with the added component of controlling the air temperature, humidity, and air movement to expedite the process. Most all commercially available lumber has been through a kiln drying process. Many times, hardwoods are given the opportunity to air dry for a few weeks before kiln drying begins to allow some of the free water to escape. There are two categories of kilns: artificially heated and controlled kilns and solar kilns, which use the natural power of the sun. Solar kilns are typically used by hobbyist or other small operations. The commercial market for small solar kilns is limited and people typically build their own. There are plenty of resources online for building your own solar kiln. Check out www.builditsolar.com/Projects/WoodDrying/wood_kiln.htm for a list of various plans.

Air drying is the most common way you'll find yourself drying out raw wood. This method involves letting the natural process take its course. Of course, there's more involved than just dropping your freshly milled lumber anywhere and coming back in a year to check on it. There are a lot of things that you can control in this process, so follow the best practices to get the most out of your material.

Preparing timbers to aid in air circulation around stacked wood

# BEST PRACTICES FOR SEASONING

You've heard some of the basics about drying lumber, but let's discuss the specific steps to proper seasoning.

## STEP 1
### CHOOSE A LOCATION FOR YOUR STACK

A good foundation is fundamental to keeping the quality of your raw wood high at the end of the seasoning process. Ideally, you should have planned the location and built your foundation before your lumber is milled. Remember, the moment after milling occurs, the drying process begins, often very rapidly, so every hour matters. Choose a location that is flat and shaded. Extra space in a garage or a shed can serve well. If outdoors, try to choose a place without too much wind exposure for the sake of stack stability to avoid extreme swings in the drying speed.

## STEP 2
### PREPARE A FOUNDATION

The actual foundation should keep the lumber several inches off the ground to protect from rot. Lay three large timbers across the area you intend to build the stack, one at each end and another in the middle. Place two long timbers along the length of the pile. These two timbers should be made straight and level using shims. Across these two long boards, place crosspieces every 18 to 24 inches (45.5 to 61 cm). If you are drying boards 1 inch (2.5 cm) or less in thickness, place the crosspieces every 12 inches (30.5 cm). Your boards will never be flatter than the foundation, so take some time to think this out and make it right.

## STEP 3
### STACK THE PILE

Place your first board on the foundation. For slab cut wood, you should stack the slabs in the order they were cut from the tree. For dimensional cut lumber, you can make your stack from 2 to 4 feet (61 to 122 cm) wide, starting with the longest boards at the bottom of the stack. Between every layer of lumber, place stickers across the width of the pile. Place crosspieces directly above the foundation so all the weight is distributed along those large timbers. Make sure that the stickers all line up nicely as your stack grows.

The stickers are important for two reasons. Their primary function is to enable airflow to all surfaces of the wood, ensuring steady, even moisture loss. Weight distribution is the other critical job of the stickers, allowing the weight to be transferred evenly down through the stack and into the ground without putting undue stress on any one area, which might result in distortion.

When the lumber is all on the pile, put some heavy cinder blocks or other heavy objects on the top layer. The added weight can help counteract some of the warping.

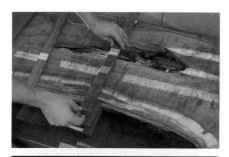

Placing stickers between slabs

Covering stacks of wood to shade them from the direct sun

## STEP 4

### PROTECT THE STACK FROM WEATHER

Direct sun can ruin drying lumber. Too much wind on a hot, dry day can do the same. Frequent exposure to rain can cause rot, fungus, or other undesirable effects. To protect from the sun and rain, you can place corrugated roofing or something similar on top of the stack. Make sure you overhang on the ends and sides and slope them to allow rainfall to run off.

The best way to control wind was back when you chose the location of the stack. Stacking next to a wall significantly decreases the velocity of air moving through the stack. If you can't do that, a makeshift lean-to will do a great job, or even a piece of plywood leaning on the side of the pile will do the trick. If you live in an arid climate, tarping can be considered for extreme circumstances, but should usually be avoided, especially when the log has just been cut. Mold and fungus will quickly grow in a warm moist environment with low airflow. Remember, you must have air movement to dry out the wood, so elimination isn't the goal, simply regulation, especially in the beginning. Later in the drying period, you can even add fans to blow air evenly through the stack to help speed up the process.

Despite being covered, air flow is still very important.

## STEP 5

### MONITOR THE MOISTURE

This step is about waiting patiently
. . . or impatiently, if you are like me.
You can monitor the moisture using a
commercially available moisture meter
if you are curious, but if you can, just let
it sit for as long as possible. If you don't
need to mess with it for a couple years,
just let it be. During the first couple of
weeks, you might look over the ends of
larger slabs for large checks, which are
stress fractures. To keep those from
spreading down the board, you can drive
some heavy-duty electrical staples on
either side of the crack. If you have been
patient and waited for a couple years,
you can be confident that it'll be well
seasoned and ready to use. On the other
hand, if you want to use it as soon as it's
ready, you will need to track the progress
with the moisture meter and wait until
you are below the 10 percent threshold
throughout the board. Before working
with the wood, bring it into the shop, or
wherever you'll be shaping it, and let it
acclimate for a few days or weeks.

Dry mesquite slabs

Checking the wood's drying progress with a moisture meter

## STEP 6

### BUILD SOMETHING

Hopefully, your first time air-drying
lumber will go more smoothly than mine.
The likelihood is that you will be met
with some failure, some success, and the
realization that you have a lot to learn.
The steps may seem simple enough, but
seasoning is so dependent on species,
climate, and a million other subtleties
that you can only pick up with experience.
Rest assured, even if your wood fights
you at every step, splits in a dozen places,
and warps with a passion, the beauty
is still there, so push forward and make
something great from it. We'll discuss
how to remedy any flaws that appear in
your wood in the projects that follow.

# PART THREE

# CRAFTING AND BUILDING PROJECTS

## CORE SKILLS YOU'LL LEARN

You'll learn the following skills by completing each of the projects in this book:

Carving

Smoothing/sanding

Cutting curves

Dimensioning boards

Sketching and designing

Boring (drilling)

Incorporating hardware

Gluing and clamping

Routing

Filling voids

Flattening boards and large slabs, including warped material

Basic joinery, interlocking joinery, mortise and tenon, butterfly joints, and supporting joinery with hardware

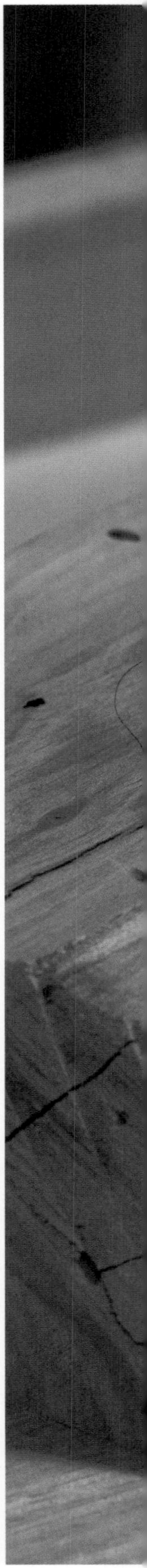

# THE BOTTLE OPENER

Carving is one of the easiest ways to shape wood into something useful. Every time I pick up a carving knife, I can't help but think about sitting around a campfire shaping a stick. Silas and I both grew up carving without any sort of formal training. While nothing much more than a fire poker came from that, with a few techniques, a sharp knife, and soft wood, it's easy to create something fun and useful like a bottle opener.

For this project, I'm using a small block of Aleppo pine. Traditionally, carvers select soft woods with a uniform grain, like basswood. My Aleppo pine is rather hard for a pine and has a swirling grain, but that's okay; I chose Aleppo because that's what grows in the desert where I live. This is a great opportunity to try any sort of wood you have around you. Small unique pieces of wood can turn a simple bottle opener into a prized tool.

Hand carved bottle opener

## PROJECT SCOPE

Get ready for a lazy afternoon's diversion.

## CORE SKILLS

Carving

Smoothing

## MATERIALS

Wood block, roughly 8 × 8 × 1 1/2" (20.5 × 20.5 × 4 cm)

Sandpaper (150)

2 coins

Tung oil (or other finish) and rag

## TOOLS

Bandsaw, small scrollsaw, reciprocating saw, or handsaw

Carving knife

Spokeshave

Rasp

Power drill

3/4" (19 mm) Forstner drill bit

Basic carving knife

Using a bandsaw to cut out the rough shape of the opener

Transferring the design from a sketch directly onto the wood block

## STEP 1

### DESIGN

As with most projects, you need to have your design down first. This bottle opener is a simple handheld model with a cutaway for the bottle cap. Sketch your design on some paper and then transfer it to the block of wood.

## STEP 2

### CUT OUT THE ROUGH SHAPE

With the design transferred to the block, use a bandsaw to cut the rough shape of the opener. Be sure to always use eye protection when using a saw and always keep your fingers far from the blade. Use a push stick to finish pushing the cuts through the saw. If you don't have a bandsaw, you could use a small scroll saw or a reciprocating saw. If using a reciprocating saw, be sure to clamp your piece of wood down securely to your workspace. You can even get by with a handsaw to get the rough shape.

Carve with a scissor motion, pulling the knife towards your thumb. Carving should produce long curls of wood.

Using a spokeshave to round the corners of the rough blank

## STEP 4
### CARVING

With the largest sections of excess material removed, begin to carve, using a basic straight bladed carving knife, which should be razor sharp. Do not underestimate these tools. With your free hand in a leather glove and a leather thumb guard on your knife hand, pull the knife toward your thumb. Don't try to move your arm; just close your hand like you would with a pair of scissors. Make small shallow strokes until you get the feel of the wood. Take a seat—carving is a relaxing activity, which is good because it takes a while. Continue carving until you're happy with the overall shape.

Using a rasp to further refine the shape.

## STEP 3
### REFINE THE ROUGH SHAPE

With the rough shape cut with a saw, use the rasp and spokeshave to further break down the block into the round shape you're after. This is a good opportunity to put the block in a vise and work on it from there. Using the two tools, you can round off the hard edges of the block. The purpose of this step is only to lessen the amount of bulk material that needs to be removed. If you're a purist (and your forearms are up to it), you can skip this step altogether.

## FEEL THE GRAIN

Learn how wood grain behaves. Make long smooth curls of wood with slow, deliberate strokes. Notice how it feels to cut with the grain and how it feels when you cut against the grain. Notice how the wood either sheers or chips depending on which direction you cut. You'll feel the same pressures of the wood grain regardless of the tool you use.

A Forstner bit ready to drill the slot for the coins

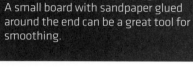

Flexible sandpaper can be especially useful to smooth over carving marks. A small board with sandpaper glued around the end can be a great tool for smoothing.

## STEP 5
### DRILL THE COIN HOLE

When you're happy with the overall shape, drill the hole for the coins. The coins will go under the bottle cap and do most of the work to pry the cap from the bottle. This project uses two pennies. A Forstner bit is best for this because it will leave a flat-bottomed hole in the wood.

## STEP 6
### SMOOTHING

At this point, it's time to make some decisions about smoothing. For this opener, almost all the carving marks are smoothed out. You may choose to keep more carving facets or maybe go all the way and smooth over everything. For a simple, handmade look, start smoothing with 150-grit flexible sandpaper. The flexible sandpaper is great for all the round shapes on this piece. A great idea is to take strips of traditional sandpaper and glue them to a small stick of wood. These little sanding sticks are great for corners or the flat sections of the opener.

The finished coin slot

## STEP 7

### ATTACH THE COINS

When the opener is smoothed to your liking, attach the coins. Drill a hole straight through the two coins and apply a dab of two-part epoxy onto the base of the hole before attaching them with a brass screw. Be sure to clamp the coins down well when you drill them through. Drill a pilot hole in the wood for your screw. Select a drill bit that's slightly smaller than your screw so that the screw still has some wood to hold onto.

## STEP 8

### APPLY THE FINISH

With the screw attached, the opener is ready for a finish. Apply tung oil to protect the wood and bring out some of the grain. Gently rub the oil over the surface of the wood until you have an even coat. When the oil dries, it creates a hard barrier to keep the bottle opener from discoloring with use.

### CHEERS!

Crack open a cold and refreshing beverage. Enjoy.

Putting the opener to its highest and best use

This project only takes a few hours, with a cold beverage to look forward to at the end.

# THE POSTER FRAME

Applewood selected for making our poster frame

Several years ago, my little brother had just moved into a place of his own. He had some posters he wanted to hang, but hoped to move beyond the thumbtacks and tape. He asked me to make him some simple magnetic, wooden poster frames, which gave the feeling of a floating poster. A handcrafted poster frame made from wood you mill yourself adds a personal touch to the poster you proudly display and is a great entry-level project for learning how to dimension boards to the final size, the basics of wood drilling, as well as sanding and finishing.

Minimalist poster frame

## PROJECT SCOPE

A few hours in the shop ought to do it.

## CORE SKILLS

Dimensioning boards

Boring (drilling)

Smoothing

## MATERIALS

1 or 2 boards of raw wood at least 1/2" (13 mm) thick, 4" (10 cm) wide, 16–24" (40.5–61 cm) long

3/8" × 1/16" (9.5 × 1.5 mm) rare earth magnet

Two-part epoxy

Sandpaper (80, 120, and 180)

Tung oil (or other finish) and rag

Adhesive wall hanging strips

## TOOLS

Table saw (or other saw capable of ripping boards)

Jointer (or hand plane)

Straight edge

Power drill (hand or freestanding drill-press) with 1/8" (3 mm) bit and 3/8" (9.5 mm) Forstner bit (ideal)

Sanding block

## STEP 1

### SELECT THE WOOD AND CUT TO ROUGH LENGTH

Perhaps the most important step of the whole process is choosing your raw boards. Since each final piece will only be 3/4 inches (19 mm) wide by 18 to 24 inches (45.5 to 61 cm) long, depending on the size of the poster you want to hang, and about a half inch (13 mm) of thickness, you need to find pieces relatively free of cracks, knots, and other defects that could impact the strength. It would be a shame for your piece to break in the middle of making it.

Once you have found the pieces you like, cut the boards to the rough length of the final frame. Rough means that you leave a little extra, from 1/2 to 1 inch (13 to 25 mm), to make your final cuts more precise later. When choosing where to trim, look for the part of the board with the fewest structural defects and trim around it. With raw wood, you'll commonly find that the ends on either side have small cracks where the wood has split during the drying process. These should be trimmed off when building something small like this. For our project, we are making a frame 18 inches (45.5 cm) wide since the poster is 16 inches (40.5 cm) wide, leaving 1 inch (2.5 cm) of overlap on each side. Add 2 inches (5 cm) to your poster width to account for overlap.

Rough trimming can be done with a handsaw, handheld jigsaw, or chop saw. Mark the cut line with pencil and double check the measurement before cutting.

Cutting the rough boards to rough length with a handsaw

## STEP 2

### CUT THE WOOD STRIPS

Using a table saw, cut 3/4-inch (19 mm) strips from the boards. One of the edges of the board must be straight before running it through a table saw. The rough milled side may be straight enough for this purpose; if not, use a circular saw along with a clamped guide board to create that straight edge. If you don't have a table saw, you can use a circular saw to cut the strips, though it takes a bit longer to set up each cut. A bandsaw could also be used for this purpose, but you will find the cut is rougher and will need more smoothing later.

Cutting the first strip on the table saw. In this case, since we are cutting a thin strip of wood, the overhead blade guard has been removed, but note that the splitter is in place and the use of a push stick.

Using a clamped guide and circular saw to cut a strip by hand

## STEP 3
## CUT THE STRIPS TO FINAL LENGTH

Once the strips have been cut, trim the pieces down to the final length using a fine-tooth crosscut saw or a chop saw. If cutting by hand, make sure to mark your cut well so you can follow the cut line as you go. If using a chop saw, a handy tip for making fine cuts is to apply masking tape to the area being cut. This supports the wood as the saw passes through the back of the material, preventing tear out. You will want to carefully choose where to cut on both ends, cutting around any defects that may have been created during the earlier steps. These are your final cuts, so make sure you get them right.

Making the final cuts with a fine-toothed pull saw

Using masking tape to reduce tear out

The wood strips cut to their final dimensions

## STEP 4

### SMOOTH

Using 80-grit sandpaper, smooth out the saw marks. In this first pass, grouping the wooden strips together allows for a consistent sanding across the strips.

## SAFETY TIPS

Hands and moving power tool blades shouldn't mix, so keep your hands away from the blade. Always make sure you use a push stick at the end of your cuts. A push stick can be made from a piece of scrap wood in a matter of minutes.

Do not stand directly behind the blade. Push the work piece at a measured pace, not too fast, but not stopping. Make sure that the work piece pushes all the way through the cut until it is completely clear of the blade.

Your table saw should have a splitter behind the blade. This will greatly reduce the tendency for a work piece to become misaligned between the blade and fence, which causes the kickback. Modern saws come with this splitter in the form of a riving knife, but if you have an older saw without a splitter, be sure to either outfit it with one or get a new saw.

All the safety measures that came with the saw should be in place, and you should wear eye, ear, and lung protection.

Rough sanding the wood strips together for consistent thickness

Measure and mark holes.

Masking tape can be used as a guide for how deep you need to drill.

Drill holes with a Forstner bit.

## STEP 5

### MARK AND DRILL HOLES FOR THE MAGNETS AND MOUNTING

Now that the strips are prepared, mark holes for the magnets. Our marks were 2 inches (5 cm) in from the outside edge and a third centered in the frame. Group each pair together and use a square to draw the pencil across both faces so the marks match on both. Using a ruler, measure halfway in across the width and make a cross hatch to mark exactly where to drill.

Carefully drill each hole to a depth slightly deeper than the magnets so that the face of the magnet will not stick out past the face of the wood. A 3/8-inch (9.5 mm) Forstner bit is the best bit for this task. It will cut a very clean hole, which makes for a more pleasing result, and has a point at the center, which makes it easy to put the hole exactly where you want it. The point of a traditional bit tends to shift slightly when first starting, causing the hole to be slightly shifted one direction or another.

A bit of masking tape on the drill bit to mark the depth of the final cut will help you drill all the holes to the same depth.

Use a drop of epoxy to hold the magnets in the holes.

## STEP 6

### INSTALL THE MAGNETS

Mix together a small amount two-part epoxy and put a drop into the bottom of each hole before inserting the magnets. Be careful to put the magnets in the proper direction when installing, with the polarity of each set to attract the magnet on the opposite face.

A sanding block is a great choice for rounding edges.

## STEP 7
### SAND

Rounding the edges of each piece by sanding at an angle will protect from future splintering and give a more polished look to the final project.

Now that all the pieces are in place, finish the sanding process progressing through first the 120-grit then the 180-grit paper. There's not much need to continue past 180, but if you find sanding to be enjoyable, continue to 220-grit. Sanding with the direction of the grain will help hide any scratches left by the sandpaper.

## STEP 8
### FINISH

Applying an oil finish will bring out the grain of the wood, as well as seal and protect the wood for longevity. First, clean off the dust from the sanding process with a clean rag. Once clean, use a new cloth to liberally apply oil. Use a second cloth to remove the excess oil and to polish with a quick buffing motion.

## STEP 9
### MOUNT

After the oil has dried, hang the back pieces using a level and adhesive hanging strips, secure your favorite poster between the magnets, step back, and enjoy a job well done.

Apply tung oil with a disposable rag.

Minimalist poster frame

THE PINEWOOD CLASSIC
ADULT-ONLY PINEWOOD DERBY RACE

### SAFETY TIP

Never pile up or throw used finishing rags in the trashcan. This can result in spontaneous combustion, due to the chemicals oxidizing in close contact. Always follow the disposal instructions on the label of the finish. I tend to hang the rags individually around the edge of the trashcan with plenty of room to safely dry. Once dry, the rags can be disposed of like normal.

# THE MINIMALIST SHELF

Repurposing some raw wood into a simple, attractive, and practical shelf can make a great addition to your home. This shelf consists of two simple pieces taken from the same board, joined together to form an L shape, and incorporates rare earth magnets to hold key rings. The mounting screws are covered up by another set of magnets, giving the shelf a minimal yet polished appearance. This project is a great introduction to joining pieces of wood together, flattening small boards, and sketching out a project plan.

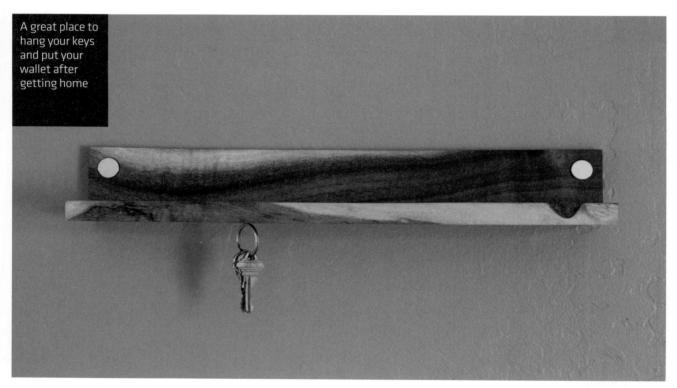

A great place to hang your keys and put your wallet after getting home

## SKETCH THE PROJECT

Sketch a plan for your shelf. Include dimensions for each piece. Our shelf ended up being 17 1/2 inches (44.5 cm) long, 3 inches (7.5 cm) tall, and 4 1/2 inches (11.5 cm) deep.

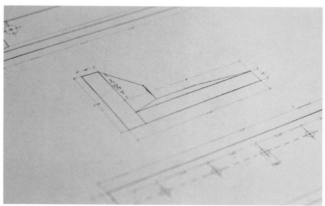

Detailed sketches of the shelf

## PROJECT SCOPE

Settle in for a Saturday well spent.

## CORE SKILLS

Flattening boards

Sketching project design

Basic joinery

Gluing/clamping

## MATERIALS

1 or 2 raw boards, 6–10" (15–25.5 cm) wide and 18–24" (45.5–61 cm) long

¼" (6.5 mm) fluted wooden dowels

Five 3/8" × 1/16" (9.5 × 1.5 mm) round rare earth magnets

Two 3/4" (19 mm) round magnets

2 wood screws with drywall anchors

Sandpaper (80, 150, 180, and 220)

Finish (tung oil)

## TOOLS

Circular saw (or table saw)

Hand plane (or jointer)

Planer (optional)

Hand drill

¼", 3/16" (6.5, 5 mm) drill bits

3/8", 3/4" (9.5, 19 mm) Forstner bits

Pull saw

Clamps

Sander

# SKETCHING PLANS

Having a sketched plan will give you a reference as you work—helpful even for a simple project like this. With more advanced projects, it is vital. I use a simple 3-D modeling program called SketchUp (available at www.sketchup.com), which has the advantage of being free. If you can draw a relatively straight line, hand drawn sketches work as well. There isn't one correct way of creating a project plan, but typically a good sketch includes information on the dimensions of each piece, location and size of holes, and more detailed drawings where joints and other features may go. Essentially, it's a way of assessing your project before you begin building and a way to remember details when you are in the thick of it. During the planning stage, I often realize a problem with my concept as I think through how I'll make each cut, and a detailed, sketched out plan is a good resource to go back to. If you think you might want to build the project again, make sure your sketch and notes are detailed so you can refer to them later.

The mesquite slab we're starting with

### STEP 2

## CUT THE PROJECT BOARD

When starting with a larger slab of raw wood, you are more likely to have significant warping from the drying process. In a later project, we will deal with flattening entire slabs, but since our shelf is intended to be small, the most efficient use of material is to cut what we need out of the slab and flatten that piece, rather than the whole thing.

Flattening across the entire slab would require removing (and wasting) more material, whereas a smaller piece will have less warping to repair, resulting in less waste.

A great tool for cutting a slab of wood is a circular saw with guide rail. Ideally, use a model designed to sit on top of its own specially made guide, but any circular saw should work if you have a guide to keep your cut on a straight path. Cut out a piece of the slab with a healthy margin for error.

Using a track saw to trim the slab

Our trimmed piece of mesquite

Checking the flatness of the wood

Using a hand plane to flatten the wood

## PREPARE THE BOARD

Once the board has been rough trimmed, it's time to correct any twist, bowing, or cupping present. Hopefully, you don't have too much, but regardless, rough sawn boards should have at least two flat reference surfaces, including one face and one edge. Nature rarely cooperates perfectly in providing this, so we must force the board to give us what we want.

Starting with the face, look for any obvious high spots. A straight edge can help with this. With a hand plane, work on taking those high spots down.

Next, you'll need to get rid of any twist present. Winding sticks are helpful with this. Essentially, these are just a pair of straight sticks placed on either end of the board. When looking down the board, they magnify any twist in the board. Working diagonally from high corner to high corner, remove the twist with a hand plane, again getting it down until it's as flat as you can make it. You'll likely need to assess the board again for any high or low areas and flatten those with another pass with the hand plane. Note that your board may never be truly flat. The more experienced you get at this process, the flatter the board will get. But don't expect perfection on your first time.

Once the face surface is flat, plane down the opposite side until the board is the desired thickness. If you have the luxury of having access to a thickness planer, this is the perfect time to use it. In this case, I'm taking off the minimum amount necessary to make the board nice and flat on both sides.

Using the bandsaw, resaw the board down the center edge so you end up with two nearly identical boards. Any skills you picked up when milling with your bandsaw will come in handy for this task. Now that you've got your final boards, do your fine trimming down to the final dimensions. This project preserves a tiny bit of live edge from what was the exterior of the tree. This is purely a design choice that many feel draws attention to the memory of the tree the wood came from. Sometimes, this technique can become heavy handed, but when applied tastefully it can be a great way to bring some personality to your work.

Using two boards as winding sticks to check for twist

Using a push stick to guide the board through a table saw

Resawing with a bandsaw

Drilling holes for the dowels that will join the two pieces

The thickness planer tool is one of the best additions I've made to my workshop.

## STEP 4

### DRILL THE DOWEL HOLES

This shelf is simple, but its single joint is important to consider nonetheless. Because the back of the shelf won't be visible, the dowel holes can be drilled through the back. Clamp the two pieces together and to a stable surface. Drill four evenly spaced holes through the back and into the shelf with a 1/4-inch (6.5 mm) bit.

## DRILL THE MAGNET AND MOUNTING HOLES

To preserve the clean aesthetic of the final shelf, we need to hide the mounting hardware, which means the mounting screws need to be countersunk and covered up with something more pleasing. In this case, we will be using larger magnets.

The placement of the two mounting holes is on the top corners of the board. With a 3/4-inch (19 mm) Forstner bit, drill down approximately 1/16 of an inch (1.5 mm) to create the space for the magnet.

With a 3/8-inch (9.5 mm) Forstner bit, drill in the center of the larger hole to create enough space for the mounting screw's head.

With a 3/16-inch (5 mm) bit, drill completely through the back of the board, allowing the mounting screw to pass through.

Create the hollows for the magnets underneath the lip of the shelf. Mark a 3/8-inch (9.5 mm) Forstner bit with masking tape to a depth slightly deeper than the magnets so that the face of the magnet will not stick out past the face of the wood. Carefully drill five evenly spaced holes in the underside of the shelf.

The holes for mounting and magnets

Test fitting the two pieces

## THERE ARE A FEW WAYS TO HANDLE JOINTS:

Use hardware, such as screws and bolts.

Use wooden fasteners, such as dowels, to pin the pieces together along with wood glue.

Shape the pieces in such a way as they nest together in what is called joinery, also in combination with wood glue.

There's nothing wrong with using hardware, but when possible, I always like to rely on dowels and joinery in my projects, and in this case, I have elected to use dowels.

## STEP 6

### INITIAL SANDING

Since the shelf hasn't been assembled yet, this step might raise an eyebrow. There's a good reason for it, however. Pre-sanding components before assembly can make the task of sanding later much easier, as you don't have to sand as much in tight corners and difficult-to-reach places. This will improve the quality of the sanding as well. There will need to be some additional sanding done at the end of any project, but having the components pre-sanded will make a big difference during those last stages. Sand all faces with 80-grit, and then 150-grit sandpaper.

## STEP 7

### GLUE THE PIECES TOGETHER

Just applying the glue and sticking the pieces together is not enough. To achieve adequate strength, joints in wood should be clamped after the glue has been applied. You can never have enough clamps in your shop. Clamping can be tricky, so before you begin applying glue, try to dry fit the pieces together and add the clamps. Mentally note where each clamp should go so you can get them on quickly once your glue has been spread.

Apply glue to the dowel holes and the edge of the shelf. Insert the dowels into the shelf (tap with a mallet if necessary to seat) and attach the back. Clamp immediately and wipe off any excess glue with a damp rag.

## GLUING TIPS

In woodworking, gluing pieces of wood together is a routine activity. There are some tricks to be aware of when starting out:

Don't drown the wood with glue. Just enough to coat the surface of the wood evenly will be fine.

Always be aware of joints that will be visible when applying the glue. By carefully applying, you can minimize the amount of glue that ends up on the outside of that visible joint.

Clean up any glue left behind. This can be difficult once it dries. This is best done with a slightly dampened rag. If there is a large quantity of glue, try to scrape it off before wiping the residue off.

Clamp together after gluing.

## INSTALL THE MAGNETS

Mix a small amount of epoxy. Apply a small drop of epoxy to the bottom of each hole before inserting the magnets. A toothpick is a good tool for this step.

## CLEANUP AND FINAL SANDING

Sanding may not be the most rewarding part of any project, but with the sanding done earlier, some 180-grit sandpaper makes short work of any remaining roughness. Live edges can be cleaned up with some steel wool or similar abrasive pads. Finish with 220-grit sandpaper at the end.

Steel wool is great for cleaning up a live edge.

Using an orbital sander to clean up dried glue

## STEP 10
### FINISH

Lastly, apply some tung oil or other similar finishes, such as Danish oil or a rub-on polyurethane gel, and let dry.

## STEP 11
### INSTALL

Using some screws and drywall anchors, install the shelf in or near your entryway. Little touches can make a big difference, and this little shelf adds a unique accent to your home and comes in handy as you come and go.

Applying a classic and durable tung oil finish

Finished shelf with keys hanging from the bottom magnets. The magnets on the top cover the mounting screws.

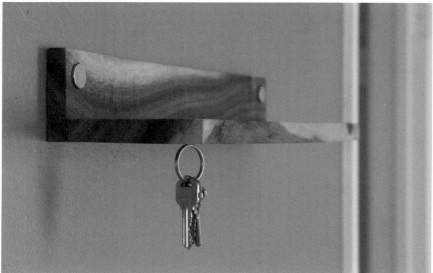

# THE SERVING TRAY

In *Felled*, we talk a lot about gathering together to share a meal. Gathering together with friends and family offers a few moments of sanity in today's busy world. Small touches like a home-cooked meal or personal and familiar environment bring even more warmth to these gatherings. A handmade serving tray can add just such a personal touch. The story of where you find your own log and how you transform it will make for a great conversation piece.

A serving tray is a great project to pick up a few important skills, yielding a piece that you can find many uses for. I can guarantee that every time you use this tray, you'll find pleasure in seeing your handiwork put to good use. A few years back, I made a serving tray, and it feels great to use it to share a meal with my family.

Acacia serving tray

## PROJECT SCOPE

Start serving food in style by dinnertime.

## CORE SKILLS

Joining boards together

Router techniques

Fine sanding

## MATERIALS

2 to 3 seasoned boards 4–6 inches (10–15 cm) wide and 12–20 inches (30.5–51 cm) long

Moisture-resistant food-safe wood glue

Sandpaper (80, 120, and 220)

Food-safe finish (mineral oil or blended mineral oil/beeswax)

## TOOLS

Circular saw

Jointer (or hand plane)

Straight edge

Bar clamps

Plunge router

Router bits: straight, flat bottom, or bowl

Hand chisel

Hand sander (or sanding block)

Stacked acacia boards

### STEP 1

## DESIGN YOUR TRAY

Since serving trays are not meant to be large, you can start out with quite a small log. Small logs like these can be easily found, moved, and milled, all in a simple home shop using basic tools. I've chosen to make a serving tray that's approximately 10 inches (25.5 cm) by 16 inches (40.5 cm) after milling the log. Many trays are 12 inches (30.5 cm) by 18 inches (45.5 cm) to accommodate two dinner plates and the necessary utensils. Others are as small as 6 inches (15 cm) by 12 inches (30.5 cm) for a small loaf of bread or cheese and fruit. Choose a size that works for you and that can be made easily from your starting log.

Deciding how to join the base of the tray

### STEP 2

## SELECT THE WOOD

Once you've ensured your boards are nice and flat, select two of your choice pieces or three pieces if you wish to make the tray a little wider. In my case, my acacia boards have some light colored sapwood next to some really striking grain. One way you can highlight features like this is to use what's called a "bookmatch," selecting two boards that came from right next to each other in the log and opening them up like a book so the grain is mirrored. This technique is nearly impossible to do if working with store-bought lumber and really makes your piece unique.

Flattening sides with a jointer

## STEP 3

### JOIN THE BOARDS

After selecting the boards, join them together to make one single board.

Use a jointer or hand plane to square the edges of the selected pieces that will be glued together.

If you don't have access to either a jointer or a hand plane (or you have a hard time with the hand plane), use a circular saw with a sharp, high quality ripping blade. Clamp the guide to the board you're cutting to run the saw against. The straighter, the better, as any deviations will show up in your joint later. Secure the boards tightly to prevent kickback.

If your saw or jointer is slightly out of square, simply joint one board, and then joint the other board in the opposite direction, alternating the pattern. If your tool is consistent in being out of square, when you flip that board you'll end up with a perfectly flat joint, even if the joint isn't perfectly perpendicular to the surface. You've probably chosen boards carefully to expose your favorite side to the top of the tray, so when using this trick, be mindful of what direction you want to be the face.

Flattening edges with a hand plane

# TIPS FOR JOINING BOARDS

If you spend any time woodworking, you'll often need to join multiple boards together to make a bigger surface. It's a no-brainer really, and you see this technique used everywhere. Even though it is common, it's trickier than it looks. To have a nice tight joint with no gaps, you need a straight, flat surface on the board's edge that's perpendicular to the face of the board (we call that square). Once you've got that on one board, you must do the same thing on the other, and they must match. It seems so basic, but sometimes the basics are tough to master. Fear not, for the shorter the board, the easier it is to get right, and serving trays are relatively small. Your first few times using this technique will likely have imperfections, and that's okay.

Checking for square

The best tool for flattening the edges of the boards you'll join is called a jointer. These machines are often found in home shops in smaller bench-top sizes and essentially consist of a cutter head (like a planer's cutting head) set between two beds, which are offset, with the bed on the right set lower than the bed on the left. The larger the offset, the deeper the cut will be. Standalone machines give you a few advantages, the biggest being a longer bed for the board to glide along. The longer the bed, the more uniform the surface will tend to be.

A hand plane can also be used to flatten the edges you'll join. Like most things with hand tools, there is a lot more skill required to get the job done just right. That takes practice, so don't be surprised if the hand plane gives you some trouble until you get the hang of it. A shooting board is a common jig (a custom tool made for a specific task) that can help ease this difficulty for you. It is used to keep your plane perpendicular to the workpiece, which ensures the edge is square once planed.

Lining up the bookmatch

Using clamps to join the slabs

Trimmed joined slabs

Applying glue

## STEP 4
### GLUE UP THE BOARDS

Once you're happy with the joint, go ahead and apply moisture-resistant wood glue to your boards. Make sure to have your clamps ready to begin placing as soon as your glue is applied. When clamping, you'll need to be prepared to face the challenge of bowing. When the bar clamps are on one side of the board, they tend to bow the entire piece out in the opposite direction. The more boards you're gluing, the more pronounced the effect. To compensate, alternate the clamps with one on bottom and one on top. Even better, use clamping cauls, which are straight stiff boards across the width of the panel. Sandwich the serving tray between the cauls and clamp them tightly. Put wax paper, plastic wrap, or masking tape on the face of the cauls to prevent them from being glued to the surface. Once the clamps are all in place, wipe up the excess glue with a damp rag.

## STEP 5
### TRIM TO SIZE

After the glue has cured, trim the boards down to the approximate final size of your serving tray.

## HOLLOW THE INSIDE OF THE TRAY

Now that the serving tray has been glued and trimmed, it's time to hollow out the inside a bit so your food doesn't fall off. If the boards clamped together unevenly, level the surface using a hand plane or sander till they are uniform. To hollow out the boards, the tool of choice is a router with a bowl bit. Use the straight edge to guide the router along the edges, using the bowl bit to achieve a bit of a curve, easing the transition from the hollow to the serving tray's edge.

Routers are difficult to operate in a straight line freehand, so it will be important to use the straight edge to provide a guide. Ensure that the workpiece and the straight edge are secured tightly onto your workbench to keep from shifting during the cut. Once you have finished cutting the perimeter, you can begin hollowing out the rest with a flat-bottomed bit. Be very careful not to bring the flat bit too close to the outside edge, as it will quickly cut into the curved slope left by the bowl bit.

Unless your serving tray is going to be quite small, the recessed portion is likely to be larger than your router's base. It is important to keep the router level and at the same elevation throughout this process or else your surface will be uneven. As you work, you will find that you are removing the surface that your router was using for support. One way to handle this is by leaving a line of uncut material every couple of inches (5 cm) to continue to support the router on. When everything is hollowed but the portions left for support, take a couple small pieces of plywood that match the depth of your hollow and place on either side of each remaining high spot, creating temporary supports that you can then run the router on top of to complete the hollow. Be sure to leave ample space between your temporary supports and the spot you intend to cut so you can avoid making contact between the bit and the support. After all this is done, you may have a few small high spots which you can cut down with a sharp chisel and bevel down so as not to gouge further into the tray.

Using a router to hollow out the middle of the tray

## STEP 7

### ADD A HANDHOLD

To make it easy to pick up the tray from a flat surface, you may want to cut a handhold on either end. This is simple to do using the same roundover bit you used earlier for hollowing. Simply mark the beginning and end point of the handhold, clamp down a straight edge for the router, and make your cut. This is a small touch that adds a lot to the finished product.

The routed handhold

Initial sanding

## STEP 8

### SAND EVERYTHING

The tray is ready for the final steps. You'll likely have some work to do to get the inside of the tray looking polished. Start with a medium 80- or 100-grit sandpaper followed by 120, then 220, and begin smoothing out any rough spots, being careful to avoid digging into the edge of the hollow. You'll probably have to sand that by hand, curving the sandpaper to follow the contour of the edge. After all this sanding, you're probably wondering why it takes so long. Don't worry, this is normal. Sanding is by far the most tedious part of woodworking, but so very important to take a project up to the next level.

## STEP 9

### APPLY FINISH TO SEAL THE PROJECT

Lastly, seal the tray to slow down and ease the natural expansion and contraction constantly occurring due to changes in ambient temperature and moisture. Serving trays are likely to be exposed to significant surface moisture and bacteria throughout their lifetime, so to make them last longer, as well as improve washability, it's important to seal up the wood pores, making it a lot harder for moisture to penetrate.

Another consideration is that it needs to be food-safe. There are lots of commercially made mineral oil blends and beeswax finishes made for just this purpose. The label will say food safe or food grade.

Hopefully, you've finished this project and are now looking at the most beautiful and functional serving tray you've ever seen. Better yet, you are serving food to friends and family on it. No matter what, you'll have a practical contrivance for years to come that reminds you daily of the rewards of your hard work.

# THE EDISON LAMP

Sometimes you come across a piece of wood full of character that just begs to be used. This happened to me as I was milling up a piece of applewood. I've already talked about the tree's background and its special meaning it has for me; I wanted to showcase this block of wood full of cracks, knots, and termite tunnels. I got to work on a custom lamp with an old-fashioned Edison bulb.

This is a great project to try out after you have experience with a few other simpler projects. This project can be created completely with raw wood milled in a small workshop and at the same time introduces a few more intricate and detail-driven skills. Incorporating hardware adds a constraint that you must design around—you can change the wood, but not the hardware. Filling voids with epoxy becomes an important skill when working with raw wood due to the many imperfections you will come across. Interlocking joinery is the hallmark of handmade quality when building fine furniture, so the more practice the better.

Throwback vintage Edison lamp made from backyard applewood

| PROJECT SCOPE | CORE SKILLS | MATERIALS | TOOLS |
|---|---|---|---|
| Clear your schedule and buckle down for a busy weekend. | Incorporating hardware | Wood | Miter saw |
| | Filling voids | Lamp socket | Bandsaw or handsaw |
| | Interlocking joinery | On/off switch | Chisels |
| | | 1/4" (6.5 mm) carriage bolts, wing nuts, and washers | Fine tooth pull saw |
| | | Fabric covered power cord | Router with router table |
| | | Solder | Straight router bit |
| | | Edison bulb | Orbital sander |
| | | Wood glue | Drill press with bits |
| | | Two-part epoxy | Stiff cleaning brush or toothpicks |
| | | Sandpaper (80, 120, and 220) | Soldering iron |
| | | Tung oil or similar finish | Screwdriver |
| | | Electrical tape | |

## SELECT AND PREPARE LAMP BASE MATERIALS

Your lamp base is likely to be the showcase of the whole piece, so find a piece with some unique character that speaks to you. It doesn't have to be an overly artistic, snobby thing; just choose a hunk of wood that looks great to you. When you have chosen the wood, try to envision the shape that works best for your wood. This is the vision stage of the project, and unlike other projects, I don't think it can easily be preplanned until you have the base in-hand. The shape my lamp took was just what felt right for my piece of wood; yours may be different.

As you envision the rough shape, begin sketching it out on the block—our final lamp ended up being about 9 x 5 x 16 inches (23 x 12.5 x 40.5 cm). When you are happy with your rough design, begin trimming away to reveal your final shape. Use a bandsaw and miter saw or a handsaw.

Cutting the angle into the back of the lamp base with miter saw

The face of the lamp base is cut with a bandsaw.

A unique applewood log milled into various pieces destined to become the lamp base

Filling voids with tinted epoxy

Silas makes a cut with the table saw.

## STEP 2

### FILL ANY VOIDS WITH EPOXY

If your wood has extra character in the form of cracks or worm holes, you might want to fill those up as shown here—or not, depending on your desired aesthetic. Filling gives them some extra contrast and make the whole thing feel a bit more refined. Clean dust and loose pieces from the voids with a stiff brush. For more stubborn debris, use a toothpick.

Using a basic two-part epoxy, fill the voids on one side of the lamp base. Give those time to set up firmly and repeat until all the sides have been filled. Make sure you wear gloves. If tint is desired, you can add it by mixing in some dye or even a bit of sawdust. If an imperfection is on the corner of the wood, the epoxy may leak out instead of staying in place. If you come across this, use some masking tape to create a form, damming in the epoxy. When the epoxy has been given plenty of time to fully cure, remove any masking tape and sand down high spots so everything is flush and smooth.

## STEP 3

### ROUGH CUT THE LAMP ARM PIECES

In the time between epoxy treatments, begin working on your lamp arms. Select some other pieces from the same log of appropriate size and characteristics. Use a table saw or bandsaw to cut them into arm-sized pieces. The two main arms should be 1 inch (2.5 cm) thick, 1 1/2 inches (4 cm) wide, and around 10 inches (25.5 cm) long, with a shorter piece around 2 1/2 inches (6.5 cm) long that the light socket attaches to.

Sanding down the excess epoxy

## CUT THE ARM-TO-BASE JOINT

The only rigid joint in this lamp is between the base and first stage of the arm. The arm fits all the way into the back of the base so that they rest flush with each other. The hollow portion of the joint needs to be cut out with an angle that matches the slight backwards sweep of the base. Mark the joint carefully on the wood with a pencil; this serves as your guide when cutting it out.

A bandsaw could be used for this cut, but because it is going to be a pretty visible joint with a unique angle, use a fine-tooth pull saw and take your time to accurately follow the marks. Once the cut has been made on either side of the joint, the material needs to be removed using a sharp chisel.

Working intelligently with the chisel makes this go quicker. Chopping through the grain is always harder than slicing into the grain from the end, so do the least amount of chopping as possible. First, score along the back of the joint by lightly striking along the line with the chisel. Once you have cut approximately 1/8 inch (3 mm) deep into the grain, give or take, move to the end of the board and use the chisel to peel off that layer of wood to the scored line. Repeat this process, moving deeper and deeper into the block each time. Once the bulk of the material has been removed, go back and clean everything up carefully until the arm fits snugly into the joint.

The rough-cut arm and base pieces laid out

Using a fine-tooth pull saw to cut the sides of the joint

The bulk of the material is removed with a sharp chisel.

## CUT THE ARM JOINTS

The movable arm joints are held together with carriage bolts, but to give a continuous visual to the lamp arm as well as to keep the bolts to a reasonable length, nest each piece with the other by removing half the thickness of both pieces where they overlap. This results in a sort of modified half-lap joint with enough material removed to allow for some rotation. This can be achieved by using various routes, including the bandsaw, handsaw and chisel, or as shown, a router on a router table. If you use a router, it's helpful to have a wide and flat bit, say 3/4 inches (19 mm), to minimize the number of passes required. Set your fence for the widest pass, which will end up being the neck of the joint,

and then beginning at the end of the arm, remove the material pass by pass. Keep the workpiece perpendicular to the fence using a miter gauge and always make sure your hands are well away from the router bit. Because this arm is rather thick and there is a lot of material to remove, I repeated this process twice, with the router bit only taking only 1/4 inch (6.5 mm) of the depth each time. This is both safer and improves the quality of the cut since it minimizes stress on the router and bit.

On the shorter lamp head piece, it is not safe to cut using this method on the router table. A handsaw and chisel are much safer alternatives. To give more freedom of rotation, trim each corner at a 45-degree angle using a miter saw.

Using a router in combination with router table and miter gauge to create the half-lap joint

## DRILL THE HOLES IN THE ARMS

Drill holes for each carriage bolt holding the half laps together and for the electrical wire to pass through. Using a drill press makes this process go a lot quicker, and the holes will be more uniform than with a hand drill, but either way should work out just fine. A Forstner bit produces the cleanest result for the lamp cord holes, which will be visible on the finished lamp.

To allow the mounting plate for the light socket to fit snugly onto the wooden lamp head piece, drill a hole on the end with a Forstner bit that matches the mounting plate. Anytime you drill a small piece like this, especially with a large drill bit, keep your hands free of the drill. Clamp it down or brace against a larger block of wood to keep your fingers out of harm's way. Drill a hole from the back of the recess to allow for the lamp wire.

Drilling a lamp cord hole with a Forstner bit

## DRILL THE HOLES IN THE BASE

Drill a hole in the base of the lamp to install the switch. Follow the specific instructions for your switch, as each has its own dimensions and specifications. Most switches require a smaller hole drilled completely through the face of the base so the switch can stick out and a wider hole for body of the switch. To make sure the smaller hole is centered within the larger, and the larger is cut to the correct depth, start the wide hole with a Forstner bit, but don't drill down

all the way. Next, using a smaller Forstner bit, use the existing center point to drill the small hole completely through the face. Complete the larger hole, slowly progressing until it is the exact depth needed. Since you have the smaller hole drilled all the way through, you can monitor your progress instead of drilling blind.

To avoid an ugly tangle of wires where the switch and power cord are soldered together, create a large recess on the underside of the base. Use a Forstner bit on the drill press to create a hollow. Alternatively, you can use a chisel. This doesn't have to look perfect since it will be hidden, but you can clean it up if you prefer. If you are using a drill bit, make sure to always start the next consecutive hole with the center of the bit with plenty of solid material to bite into, not hanging over the preexisting hole.

For the wire to get into the base and back out to the arm, drill a hole that meets up with the wiring recess and is big enough for two wires in the back of the block.

Finished arm sections. Note the reduced thickness and trimmed corners on either end of the arm.

Using a Forstner bit to drill recess for lamp socket mounting plate

Drilling the cord hole in the lamp head block

The completed two-stage hole for the light switch

The completed lamp head block, with lamp socket plate epoxied in place

## STEP 8

### SAND TO FLATTEN AND GLUE THE ARM TO THE BASE

Before the arm is attached to the base, it is a good idea to sand all the parts with 120- to 220-grit sandpaper.

This will likely be one of the simplest glue jobs you will ever do. There should be no need for clamps, so simply apply glue to the interior of the joint and to the arm. Try to avoid putting any glue within half an inch (13 mm) of the top of the joint to avoid having to clean it up later. Once the glue is dry, sand the arm completely flush with the base.

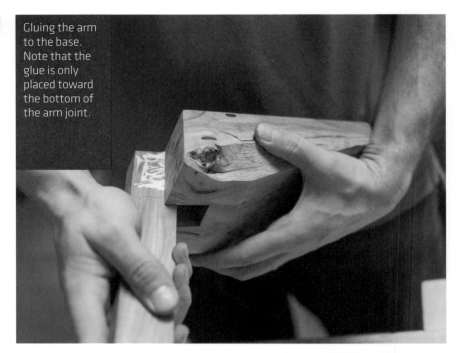

Gluing the arm to the base. Note that the glue is only placed toward the bottom of the arm joint.

A belt sander makes short work of flattening the bottom of the arm joint.

## STEP 9

### APPLY FINISH TO THE WOOD

In this project, finishing is not done as the last step. Applying the finish should be done before the hardware is installed to keep the finishing materials off the hardware. For this project, we chose a tung oil finish.

Sanding an arm piece

A simple soldering job to connect the power cord

## INSTALL THE HARDWARE AND WIRING

Install the switch, attach the adjustable arm, run the wire, and lastly connect the light socket. Make sure you follow all the wiring guides for your particular switch and light socket. Once all your hardware has been incorporated and an Edison style bulb installed, the lamp will be ready to show off in your living room.

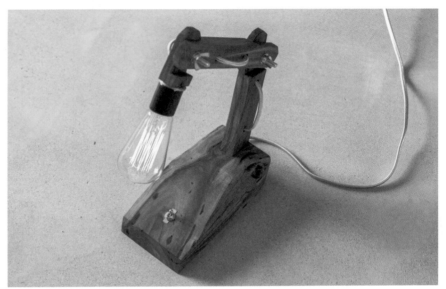

David's steady hands installing the lamp socket

# THE COFFEE TABLE

Building furniture is what first drew me to woodworking. The first coffee table I ever made was for my mom. It was a surprise gift, and I worked tirelessly, hour upon hour, to create something I was proud of. I remember the unveiling well, and the joy it gave her was well worth all the hard work.

The projects to this point have been small and technically much easier than building a piece of fine furniture. Going from making a serving tray or lamp to a coffee table may feel like a big step, and in many ways it is, but practicing with small projects gives you all the skills you need to approach a simple piece of furniture. Remember: with a good dose of patience, you will be well on your way to creating beautiful furniture.

I had a particular set of mesquite slabs in mind when envisioning this coffee table. The tree came from my neighbor's front yard. When it was removed, they simply asked the crew to leave the trunk behind for me to gather. As I was giving this tree a new life, I could step outside my shop, look across the alley, and see where it lived and died. I could also see where the logs sat and seasoned for two years, driving my wife crazy.

A mid-century influenced coffee table made from a neighborhood mesquite tree

## PROJECT SCOPE

You might just find your evenings full for a couple of weeks.

## CORE SKILLS

Flattening larger slabs

Mortise and tenon joinery

## MATERIALS

4 or 5 seasoned slabs, approximately 18" (45.5 cm) wide, 48" (122 cm) long, and 1 1/2 to 2" (4 to 5 cm) thick

Wood glue

Sandpaper (80, 120, and 220)

Finish (tung oil, polyurethane, or similar)

## TOOLS

Router and router table

Flat bottom router bit

Flattening jig for router

Thickness planer

Miter saw

Circular saw with straightedge

Fine-tooth pull saw

Chisels

Hand drill

Clamps

Handheld belt sander

Random orbit sander

A simple set of plans is vital when building furniture.

## MAKE A PLAN

Having a plan when building a piece of furniture is essential. The plan for this mid-century influenced coffee table is fairly basic: a top, four legs, and a shelf. The curveball here is that the legs are set at an angle rather than being straight up and down. It's easy to come up with a concept in your head, but the details of each joint, the angle you need to cut each piece, and a multitude of other details are precisely why it's so important to have plans. Once the plans have been created, keep them handy in the shop and refer to them frequently. This isn't to say that I always adhere strictly to the plan. As the build progresses, you may need to adapt due to material constraints or unforeseen issues. Make simple notes on the design of any changes as you go and move along. Our plans were for a table 24 inches (61 cm) wide, 42 inches (106.5 cm) long, and 18 inches (45.5 cm) high.

Slowly but surely the slab's surface is made uniform.

Checking the board's flatness with a level

The thickness planer is a big timesaver when preparing your raw materials.

# PREPARE THE RAW WOOD

The steps to preparing your raw wood are no different than for the smaller projects, just larger. The slabs you'll be working with need to be relatively flat. Flattening multiple larger pieces of raw wood by hand will have you questioning our choice in hobbies. Use this trick for flattening slabs. Create a sled for your plunge router that rests upon flat boards on both sides of the slab. The result is a track of sorts that allows your router, equipped with a wide, flat bottomed bit, to glide back and forth across the slab as you push the sled from one end to the other. Perpendicular side guides keep the router under control as you make pass after pass. Depending on the amount of warping present, you may have to do two passes: one for the highest spots and another to equalize the whole surface. Remember that multiple passes removing smaller amounts of material are better than single deep passes.

Once one side is flat, flip the slab over and repeat on the other side. Make sure that when you set your slab in place, you average out any twists by shimming opposite corners equal amounts, minimizing the material you need to remove. If your planer is large enough, trim the slabs and send them through the thickness planer, using the side you just flattened as your flat-reference. Remember, you have to have one side flat for a thickness planer to get a board square.

## CUT ROUGH PIECES

Choose the two best pieces for the tabletop and the rest for the base. The pieces that make up the base will need to have some structural strength, so cut around major defects. Use a paper template to mark each leg and avoid those problem areas. Use a circular saw with a straight edge to make these straight cuts that aren't parallel to the edge of the board. A bandsaw could be used here, but the cut will need more sanding later on to smooth all the saw marks.

The pieces making up the legs and base of the table have very specific angles that they need cut at so everything fits together nicely at the end. Use a miter saw for this, carefully reviewing every cut with your plans. This table has legs that splay out in both directions: 9.5 degrees toward the end and 6.5 degrees to the side. The top of the legs are cut at a 35.5 degree angle and 45 degrees on the upper support.

When rough trimming the slabs for the top, leave plenty of extra space to allow for some flexibility later when it is time finish the table. It's best to leave those decisions till later, after you can see the table coming together and visualize the proportions of the top next to the base.

Deciding where to trim the slabs for the tabletop

These bookmatched slabs will eventually be joined together and become the tabletop.

Silas trims a slab with a track saw.

## NOTICING PATTERNS IN THE PROCESS

By this point in the book, you may be getting a sense of deja vu, as the projects in this book tend to repeat the same basic steps. There is a natural structure that crafting with wood necessitates and that I truly appreciate. The logical progression of a project gives a framework to follow while also allowing creative choices.

A paper template being used to lay out the tapered legs

Template success! The leg matches.

### JOINERY

In this table, the cross supports on either end have traditional mortise and tenons. The mortise is a hollow, and the tenon is a matching protrusion which, when fit together, form a strong joint—even without gluing (A, B). When fit together, they form a very strong joint, even without gluing. Where the legs meet the long upper supports, an interlocking miter joint is used (C–G). Because the miter joint isn't always very strong, and in this case is such a critical structural point in the table, some large screws add an extra layer of strength. When reinforcing with screws, drill a larger relief hole to hide the head of the screw. This is what's known as countersinking (H).

Make the mortise and tenons with a router and a straight cut bit. Use the plunge router to create the hollow for the mortise and the router on a table to cut the tenons (I–K). Traditionally, this joint has square edges, but since the router naturally creates a hole with rounded corners, it can be easier to round the tenons than to square the mortises (L). You can use a handsaw and chisel to create this joint if you don't have a router.

The legs of this table are angled out slightly not only toward the end of the table but also toward the side, which creates compound miters. Every time a joint is cut, careful attention needs to be given to cut at the appropriate angle. Thankfully, a miter saw makes this much more practical than if cutting by hand (M).

The other major joint in this table is where the shelf pieces meet the cross support. The inside edge of each cross support has a supporting ledge so the shelf pieces can rest flush with the support. Later, these will be glued and pinned into place with dowels drilled in from the bottom. This will provide decent lateral support, which is the structural function of the shelf (N–Q). Having a long support piece running the length of the table midway down the legs keeps everything more stable when kids are pushing on it, adults are sitting on it, and during all manner of abuse that a coffee table receives.

### MAKING FURNITURE TO LAST

Fine furniture is built with solid joinery. This is the key difference between a cheap mass produced coffee table with screws for joints and one built to last forever. Wherever possible, it is best to design joints that nest together, giving them stability and more surface area for the glue to contact. The art of joinery adds a layer of complexity to every fine-furniture project. When it goes well, it is a joy, and when things go poorly, there are few things more frustrating.

David says that I always over-design and over-build, which I take as a compliment because the furniture I've made has held up very well. The one time I went against my better judgement, one of my dear friends broke through the top of a bench when sitting down, embarrassing both of us. Rest assured, when I repaired that bench, I made sure it was plenty strong. Follow your instincts when designing your structure, unless you have poor instincts, in which case, get a second opinion.

A completed mortise

A

A complete tenon after it has been rounded.

Using a miter gauge is a must to keep the leg secure on the router table.

A tongue and groove router bit on a router table makes quick work of the leg joint.

The groove extends only partway through the leg, to keep the joint hidden from the front.

Trimming the tongues on the top support with a fine-tooth pull saw. These will nest beautifully with the grooves cut into the legs.

Not quite mortise and tenon, not quite tongue and groove, this custom joint will be more stable than plain miter joint.

A countersunk hole for the screw head hides reinforcing hardware.

Silas cuts the tenons into the cross support with a router. A flat-bottomed bit combined with a router table is a great way to cut the shoulders of a tenon.

Using the cross support to mark out the location of the mortises.

Silas uses a plunge router with a self-centering attachment to cut a mortise.

Checking the tenon for thickness before rounding edges. If the fit is too tight, the tenon will be trimmed.

Cutting the miter angle on the legs

Laying out the spacing of the shelf pieces before cutting into the cross-supports.

A jig, concocted to use with a router when creating the recess for the shelf pieces to rest on, allows the router to be held at an angle when cutting the recess in the cross-support at the appropriate angle.

The cross support is clamped in place below the jig, with the router running above it. The result is a recess that allows the shelf pieces to rest parallel with the ground.

Squaring off the corners of the shelf support with a chisel

Silas ponders how to glue up the table base.

Silas jointing together the table top by placing the two slabs together and making a fresh cut with the track saw

## STEP 5

### DRY FIT

Before permanently gluing anything, make sure you do a dry fit, piecing everything together without adhesive. This dry fit will tell you if you've made any inadvertent errors or if you need to fine tune any of your joints. Plus, it's just great to be able to see the progress you've made. Identify each piece with a light pencil mark, to keep track of where each goes and to make sure you don't make some irreversible error later.

A very important part of the rough fit is to plan for how you will clamp the pieces up when gluing. It's a bad idea to start gluing without having any notion of where to place your clamps. Time suddenly moves faster when you start gluing, and before you know it, you'll have spent all your time fiddling with clamps and your glue will be set before everything is put together.

## STEP 6

### JOIN THE TABLETOP PIECES

Make sure the two pieces have straight and square edges so the joint will be nice and tight. Use a biscuit joiner to give some extra strength and to keep the two pieces aligned when clamping together. Or cut a channel down the center of both slabs using a router bit and cut splines to fit as shown here. Make sure that you don't cut the groove anywhere near the end of the slabs, especially if you plan on trimming more later, or else you could end up with a hole in the end of your tabletop.

Make some marks where the two pieces should meet or find a landmark to serve as your matching point and apply your glue. Remember to alternate clamps up and down to evenly distribute the clamp's force and to keep everything nice and flat.

Using the groove cutting bit on the router table to cut grooves into the edge of the slab

A completed groove. Note that the groove stops before the end of the slab.

Dry fit of custom spline pieces that will match and strengthen the two slabs together

The glue up begins by adding plenty of glue to the inserts.

Using a stick to evenly distribute glue across the surface

Glue up complete, with clamps in place

## FILL ANY VOIDS

This step will only be necessary if your wood has voids. Mesquite is full of odd holes, dark cracks, and other anomalies, so there are plenty of places that need filling on the table top. For the base, there should not be anything to fill since defects were avoided for structural integrity. The epoxy is tinted here to match the look of the wood.

Adding tint to clear epoxy

The form, which is coated with a release agent, intended to hold the epoxy is taped into place. Add modeling clay around the edges to make the crack watertight.

Pouring epoxy into the bottom of the slab

## WHEN THINGS GO WRONG

Every project brings its own adventures, no matter your experience level. Usually for me, an adventure means unexpected adversity comes along that throws a wrench my plans. This time, I tried out a new epoxy that was much thinner, with a longer cure time, thinking that it would reach all the nooks and crannies better. Indeed, it did, and actually leaked through my tape, pouring all over my floor. I was left with a mess and had to redo the entire operation. With that in mind, be careful when pouring a larger quantity of epoxy to plug up any leaks on the bottom of the board. A better way to seal the cracks is to use modeling clay to make any molds or cracks watertight and to reinforce with tape. Lesson learned.

## INITIAL SANDING

Sanding before you glue the base together will greatly improve the aesthetic quality of your final furniture. The idea is to take individual pieces and sand them before the final project has been assembled, reducing the number of hidden and impossible to reach places you'll have to sand. There's no way you can sand little nooks and crannies well, and more often than not, you'll end up scratching the surface of an adjacent piece. Since the miter joints between the legs and top supports are supposed to be flush, I treated those assemblies as a single piece and sanded after they were glued up. At the end of the initial sanding, you should have a nice tidy group of components, ready for assembly.

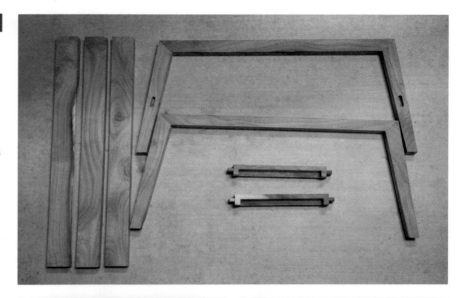

The result of all the hard work on the base joinery. These pieces are ready to be glued together.

Gluing the leg joints and using the screws in place of a clamp to hold the pieces firmly in place

Rough sanding a completed leg piece. After sanding, any irregularities in the joint are sanded flush for a clean miter joint. All the reinforcements will be hidden in the final table.

## GLUE AND ASSEMBLE

Drill countersunk screw holes from the top of the cross supports into the legs. Apply glue to the miter joints of the legs and screw together.

Use a small brush to apply glue to the inside of the mortises and the surfaces of the tenons. Assemble the legs and crosspieces and clamp in place. Use scrap wood to protect the legs from clamp indentations.

The last piece to glue involves a dowel joint, securing the shelf slats to the cross-supports. Drill the dowel joints last because things have shifted a small amount from the dry fit, and even a miniscule change makes it next to impossible to drive that dowel into place. Drill the dowel holes from the underside of the crosspiece into the shelf slats. Mark the drill bit for the correct depth so you do not drill through the shelf. Apply glue to the dowels and assemble.

Silas fits a top support to the legs during the glue up.

Drilling the hole for a dowel which will secure the shelf piece in place

## GLUE GOALS

When you are gluing the furniture framework you have two goals. First and foremost, your priority is to join the pieces together so they are rock-solid and stable. Second is to minimize the glue going places you don't want it to..We've talked about squeeze-out before, which is what you want to see when edge joining boards, but in this project, your glue shouldn't squeeze out much. The mortises should have extra depth to allow for excess glue to pool, instead of squeezing out, and glue does not need to be applied to the shoulders of the tenons, as it doesn't greatly improve the strength of the joint. If you get glue all over the place, all that work pre-sanding the pieces will have been for naught, and it will be impossible to remove all the glue. You need enough glue to get a nice bond, but you definitely don't want too much in this situation.

Trimming a dowel after the glue has dried

After trimming, the sides of the tabletop are sanded smooth.

After three hours of sanding, the table top is ready for final trimming.

## FINAL SANDING

After all the epoxy has cured on the tabletop, the final sanding step begins. Touch up any spots that need attention on the base, and if you hadn't already in the first sanding step, round the corners over a bit. Sand the table top, beginning with a handheld belt sander to remove material quickly. Once the rougher sanding has been done, any final trimming necessary can be done on the tabletop followed by the fine sanding with the orbital sander.

Sanding a table top is a time-consuming task, but as tedious as sanding is, the time and attention in this step will make itself apparent in the finished piece.

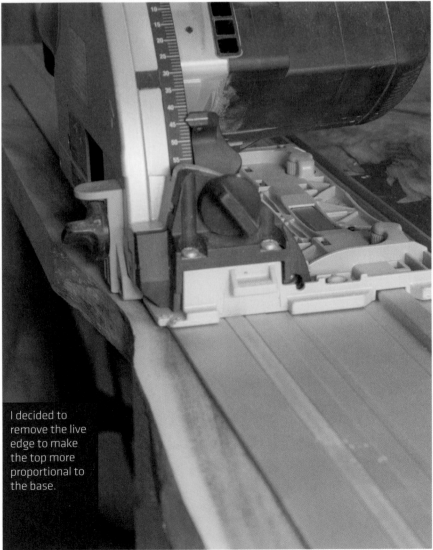

I decided to remove the live edge to make the top more proportional to the base.

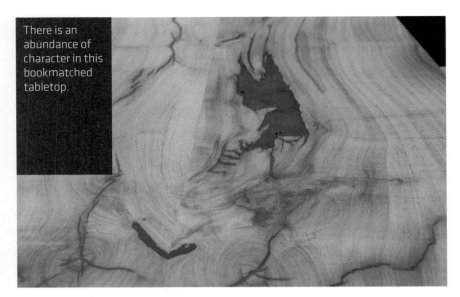
There is an abundance of character in this bookmatched tabletop.

## STEP 11
### FINISH THE BASE AND TOP

Before connecting the tabletop to the base, apply the finish. To bring out the contrast in the wood, two coats of dewaxed shellac were applied before finishing with a polyurethane on the table top to protect against moisture. Polyurethane is more resilient than oil, so for table tops, it is a good choice.

As the shellac is applied, the nuances of the wood grain are revealed.

## SHELLAC

Shellac is made from the secretions of a bug called the lac bug. Every time I use it, I wonder how the usefulness of these bugs was first discovered. Either way, I am grateful for the discovery because it reveals the subtleties of the wood grain beautifully.

The finish adds contrast to the grain.

## ATTACH THE TABLE TOP TO THE BASE

Last, but not least, attach the table top to the base using screws: one screw on each corner of the base. To allow for expansion and contraction that naturally occurs with every piece of wood, drill the holes in the base larger than the width of the screw. This will allow you to tighten the top down while allowing the small amount of side-to-side movement. It shouldn't be able to be easily shifted side to side by pushing on it, but the massive amount of force behind wood movement will easily shift the screws when it's needed.

Drill the holes in the base and then set the base upside down on the bottom of the tabletop, position in the proper place, and mark and drill pilot holes for each screw. Pilot holes should be smaller than the screw by a small margin, allowing the threads to dig into solid wood.

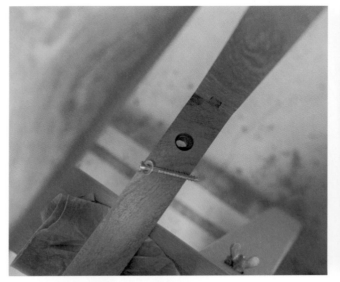

An oversized hole is drilled for the screws that mount the top to the base. This allows for the natural expansion and contraction of the wood that will occur.

## PUT YOUR FEET UP ON A FINE PIECE OF FURNITURE

Upon completion of your first piece of fine furniture, you will probably feel a unique mixture of relief and gratification. If you made any mistakes along the way (and let's be honest—you did), you will always remember where they are, but at the same time feel a sense of pride for the work you did and for what it became. No one else will notice the mistakes, or if they do, they will be too polite to tell you. Doubtless, in a few days, you will start to feel the need to begin a new piece of furniture, so in the meantime, sit back and kick your feet up on your awesome new coffee table.

Completed urban mesquite coffee table

# THE DINING TABLE

A dinner table can be the most meaningful piece for furniture you make and also the most useful. When we were trying to decide what *Felled* would be all about, we knew from the start that it needed to center around family and the place that a family always gathers is around a dinner table. I remember well the table I grew up with, a simple mission style leaf table that was handed down by my grandmother. When thinking about what I wanted in a table, I couldn't help but be taken back to memories of Thanksgivings and Easters and even just a run-of-the mill Friday night dinner around that table. Growing up, connecting and reconnecting with my family, there's just so much that can happen around a dinner table. It's a powerful statement to build a table for yourself or your family. If done right, it's an heirloom that will be passed down for generations.

We're going to build a simple and relatively small dining table with beautiful mid-century inspired design and solid joinery. Your table may look different depending on the wood you have available, but the techniques learned here could help build more memories than any other woodworking project you ever take on. While Silas has made many tables of different sizes and styles, this is the first dinner table I've made. We wanted to show what a relative beginner can do with access to a few tools and some solid techniques. Let's start this journey together on a piece that will be part of our growing families for generations.

## TOOLS

Planer

Circular/track saw

Table saw

Jointer

Chisel

Router

Drill

A good plan is important when building something as complex as a dinner table, even if it's a simple design. For my design, I decided I wanted a mid-century modern aesthetic with a boat shaped top and tapered legs. Your table should fit your style, and you will want to take your time researching the various basic styles out there and incorporating all the elements you like.

To source the wood large enough for this project, Silas and I visited our local sawmill. To learn more about milling and seasoning your own wood for this project, see the sections on milling and seasoning lumber.

Wiping away squeeze out on our mesquite tabletop

## STEP 1

### DESIGN

There are a few general rules for dining tables: Standard height is from 28 to 32 inches (71 to 81.5 cm), with 30 inches (76 cm) being the happy medium. For every seat at the table, you'll need approximately 24 inches (61 cm) of table space on the sides and enough room for someone to fit at each end, so for an eight-person dinner table, your design should be at least 6 feet (2 m) long, 36 to 42 inches (91.5 to 106.5 cm) wide, and 30 inches (76 cm) high. When designing, pay special attention to the clearance between the bottom of the table and the tops of your chairs, allowing for around 8 to 12 inches (20.5 to 30.5 cm) of space.

## ADAPTING YOUR PROJECT

When using urban lumber, your plans must be flexible to adapt to the wood available. Ideally, in every project, the finished product highlights the strengths of the log you started with and perfectly matches the pictures you had in your head—but sometimes the wood has different ideas. Be flexible so that the adjustments you make allow the wood to shine.

## SALVAGING BADLY WARPED LUMBER WITH A PLANER SLED

My table design called for a top that was 1 or 1 1/2 inches (2.5 or 4 cm) thick to help balance the top and the base. While visiting the mill, some beautiful local acacia slabs caught my eye. These slabs were heavy—8 feet (2.5 m) long and over 3 inches (7.5 cm) thick—much thicker than required for my table top.

Instead of just planing the slabs down and leaving nearly half of this special wood behind as planer chips, we decided to have them resawn down to 1 inch (2.5 cm) and 2 1/2 inch (6.5 cm) slabs on the bandsaw mill. This would give us a more manageable slab for our top and plenty of stock to make our base. We knew this approach was slightly riskier, but we couldn't bear to see the wood go to waste. We're adventurous sorts, and we were confident in our ability to adapt to any unforeseen situations—and that's good because we got ourselves into an interesting situation.

Being able to adapt to a changing situation is the name of the game with urban lumber. Based on what we knew about the history of these slabs, we believed that they should be dry, but as it turns out, they weren't dry enough. Before resawing, we took a surface moisture reading, but it seemed a little high considering the log's history. We decided to trust what we knew about the log's history instead of trusting the moisture meter, thinking perhaps it had been thrown off by recent precipitation, but within a couple weeks, the resawn slabs had badly warped.

You'll be tempted to freak out the first time you see truly warped lumber. But the important thing to remember is that with the right techniques and the right design, you can turn even the waviest boards into a beautiful piece. Our acacia slabs were ready to become something more but would never be able to produce a table top. We decided to salvage the acacia for the table base and procure three local mesquite slabs for the top.

Warped acacia slabs

Resawing an acacia slab

An urban acacia slab before being cut and flattened

Trimming a warped acacia slab

Flattening the first acacia board

Moving forward, we had to find a way to use this badly warped acacia, which required some out-of-the-box thinking. A trick we had learned about in the past was to rip the slabs into narrower sections and place the warped boards one at a time onto a flat platform (called a sled) that can travel through the planer, thus flattening the top of the warped board. Once the top is flat, it is removed from the platform, turned over, and sent through the planer again, resulting in a nice, albeit thinner, board with two flat faces. It's quick and can be done with the sort of planer that many people have in their workshop.

Practically speaking, there are many ways to build such a sled.

Build a platform. Our sled is just a piece of particleboard; yours can be anything that's flat, decently rigid, and able to fit through your planer.

Secure the board to keep it from moving. We secured ours between two braces using screws at both the end of the board so they are just barely biting into the wood. It's vital that the screws travel through the side of the brace into the end of the board so that the screws never come close to contacting the planer's cutting head.

Shim the board in areas that don't make direct contact with the platform so that the board does not flex as it moves through the planer. The planer's rollers put downward pressure on the workpiece as it travels through. During this shimming process, it's best to average the high and low spots on opposite corners to preserve the maximum thickness possible. We shimmed our board with cheap wooden door shims, hot-gluing them in place. Once the board is securely shimmed, run the whole assembly through the planer. Take small passes until all the areas of the board have been touched by the planer's blade. Once the top is flat, you can remove the board from the platform and flip it over to flatten the bottom.

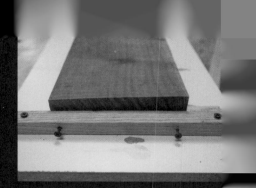

Stop blocks go on either end of the warped board with screws drilled in to the ends of the board just enough to keep the board from shifting.

When shimming a slab on our flattening sled, hot glue is great for securing the board. The hold is strong enough to keep the boards stable through the planer but easy to remove afterward.

After running on the sled, you can flip the board and run the other side.

Checking the flatness of our planed acacia

Running the longer boards for our stretcher

Eliminating warp removes a lot of material.

Flattened acacia boards for the base sitting on top of mesquite slabs for the top

STEP 2

## PREPARE THE BOARDS

Cut the components for the table to rough dimensions. Flatten and square these pieces with a hand plane as described in the shelf project (page 76), router sled as used in the coffee table project (page 100), or the planer sled method (page 118). If the boards are not square, run each board across the jointer to quickly square up one side or use a circular saw with a straight guide to cut a straight line.

Ripping our freshly flattened acacia boards

Each board is ripped in half and will be laminated together to make thicker boards.

A push stick is often an important part of safely using a table saw.

## BUILDING UP STOCK

My table base called for two crosspieces between the two sets of legs and one stretcher to run the length of the table and connect the crosspieces. I wanted the legs, crosspieces, and stretcher to be thick and solid; however, I had no materials thick enough to create those pieces. This is a common issue for woodworkers, and the solution is quite simple: Make bigger pieces by building up smaller ones.

When flattening the boards, we purposely cut the width of each board twice as wide as the final width called for in our design. For example, when we needed a 3 1/2-inch (9 cm) wide stretcher, we cut a 7-inch (18 cm) wide rough board. That way, we could later cut the flattened board in half lengthwise (known as ripping), turn the faces of the ripped board towards each other, and laminate them together, resulting in thick, solid pieces for the base of the table. Through this technique, our 2-inch (5 cm) warped slabs easily yielded enough material to build up seven perfectly flat 2-inch (5 cm) pieces.

## STEP 3

### TRIM AND LAMINATE THE PIECES

If your base requires building up stock, the next step is to laminate your boards together and trim to the final dimensions. With rough boards now prepared, you'll rip them on a table saw and glue the faces together. Set the fence on the table saw, double checking the distance from the inside edge of the blade to the fence with a ruler, and run the pieces through with the square edge against the fence.

This table base design calls for seven pieces—four identical leg pieces, two crosspieces to go between each set of legs, and the stretcher that connects the crosspieces. Take special care to choose the best-looking sides of the boards (which will face outwards in the finished table) and pair up the boards to be glued. Spread a thin layer of glue on both sides of all contacting surfaces and secure with clamps. Glue coverage is always more important than glue thickness. Squeeze the clamps tight until you get glue coming out of the joint and let dry.

Glue squeezed out of a joint has to be sanded off, but it does indicate that you have good glue coverage.

Our acacia stock ready to be laminated along with trimmings from the slab. Using boards this warped uses a lot of material.

Glued and clamped boards that will become table legs

Clamping the longest acacia boards, which will become the stretcher

Trimming the inside edge of a mesquite board for our table top. Which side of the slabs you trim can have a big impact on the table top's final width.

Generously spreading glue on each contacting face

## STEP 4

## JOIN THE TABLE TOP

While the glue is drying for the flattened, trimmed, and laminated base pieces, begin work on the table top. The mesquite slabs for this table were just about 5 1/2 feet (168 cm) long and each about 18 inches (45.5 cm) wide. Because they were too large for our small planer, we opted to take the boards to a local woodworking shop, where they have a wide planer. We discussed what we wanted with the technician and came home with beautiful, flat boards.

Decide on the best arrangement for your table top boards. For this project, the widest boards were placed on the outside, making use of the curved sides to create an elliptical shape. This common oval element in mid-century furniture is called a boat top. It's a rounded taper down the length of the table that can add some interest and offset the otherwise straight and rigid angles in the design.

Roughly trimming the end of our tabletop before joining

Remember, sometimes the best option is a solid handsaw.

Cutting both facing edges of two boards before joining is a great way to get a tight joint.

Marking the location of each biscuit on each board

We included biscuits about every 6 inches (15 cm).

Biscuits aren't just strong—they're also quick to use.

Make a mark in the middle of your biscuit to make sure they can be inserted slightly more than half way.

David clamps together the table top with several strong bar clamps.

Join the top using biscuits. Cut slots every 6 inches (15 cm) or so with a biscuit joiner along all the edges to be joined. Spread glue on one half of each biscuit and insert in a slot. Spread glue on both faces and the other half of the biscuits. Assemble the pieces and clamp, alternating the clamps above and below for balance.

As always, a dry fit without glue is important.

We don't use glue sparingly, but remember that coverage is more important than volume.

Scoring the outside of a spine on the bottom of our tabletop

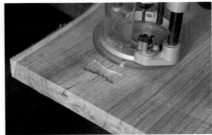

The first shallow pass cutting out the hole for our spline

Using a chisel to refine the edges of the hole

## FILL ANY VOIDS AND CRACKS

Once the top is glued, survey the top for cracks and voids. This mesquite has cracks near the ends and one large inclusion that will need attention. The inclusion can simply be cleaned out and filled with epoxy, as in the coffee table project on page 100. The cracks near the ends of the boards are a different story. Edge splits are common, and they won't just stop on their own, so they need to be stabilized with a spline to keep them from expanding further. You can get jigs and kits for cutting butterfly splines or you can cut your own freehand, as done here. Start by sketching out a bowtie shaped spline on some spare wood and cut them out on the bandsaw. Take the spline and score the outline over the crack you want to stabilize. First, use a router to cut out a rough hole, keeping a bit of distance from the scored outline, and then finish with a chisel for precise cutting. Go slowly and take a few passes with the router. This spline was 1 inch (25 mm) thick, so the hole was about 3/4 inches (19 mm) deep. Using a chisel, carefully square off the sides and corners. Check your progress by frequently dry fitting the spline. Once you can fit the spline into the hole without a large amount of force, glue the spline in place. One great way to help the spline fit is to taper the bottom of the spline with a sander.

Tracing butterfly splines on a spare piece of acacia

Completed hole for butterfly spline

Once glued into place, you can use a handsaw to cut the butterfly flush with the top.

Using a flexible piece of stock and clamps to mark the curved edges of the tabletop

The table edge was cut with a 10-degree taper. There was plenty of sanding needed to even out the jigsaw's cut.

## TRIM THE TABLETOP

Square the ends of the table. The edge on this table is cut with a 10-degree angle to make the top slightly larger than the bottom. To do this, you can set the track saw to cut in at 10 degrees and cut both ends. To create the sweeping curve from a 33-inch (84 cm) wide end to a 35 1/2-inch (90 cm) middle for the oval-shaped top, mark the center point and center width, and then set up clamps on either end. Using a flexible piece of stock, bend the stock along the edge clamps and push it out to the middle 35 1/2-inch (90 cm) mark. Secure the bowed stock in the middle with a clamp and trace the curve with a pencil. As long as your stock is a consistent thickness and centered on your tabletop, this will give you a beautiful angle. Cut the curve with a jigsaw set at the 10-degree angle. It may turn out a little rough, which is a risk when using a jigsaw, even if you're an experienced woodworker. The curve can be cleaned up with a belt sander.

A belt sander was used to roughly sand epoxy and splines before sanding on a wide sander.

## THE RIGHT TOOL MIGHT BE SOMEONE ELSE'S

Most every city has woodworking stores that cater to hobbyists and professionals. These aren't just a great place to purchase supplies and get some advice; they're often a resource for the sort of industrial-sized tool that you'd never be able to purchase for your garage or shop. Tabletops are always going to be bigger than a home planer or sander, but they fit great in the back of a pickup or minivan. You can save yourself an incredible amount of effort by leveraging the tools at your local woodworking shop.

For sanding a large piece like a tabletop, we got a wise idea to help cut down on our time spent in the workshop. We hauled our joined top back to the woodworking shop, where they had a 36-inch (91.5 cm) sander. So guess how wide we cut our table top? 35 1/2 inches (90 cm). It's always good to leave a little room on either side. Sanding the top helped to smooth out our epoxy and the small inconsistencies between the slabs. It easily saved us half a day of sanding and was even cheaper than the planing.

Sometimes, the best tool for the job is a tool that you won't have in your workshop or garage or apartment patio. That's okay. It's good to respect tools and use the right tool for the job, but in the end, a tool has to serve the project. If you find more virtue in sanding for hours, you should do that. In my opinion, you're better off spending your time working smarter, not harder.

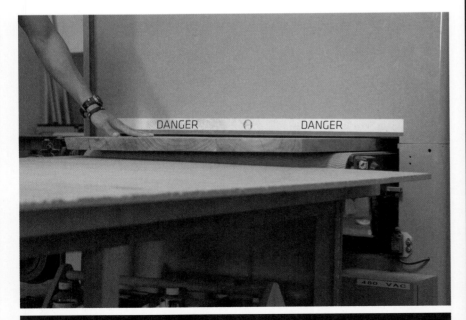

DANGER    DANGER

480 VAC

The wide sander at our local woodworking store saved us a day of work.

Squared pieces cut to length for our table base

Glued acacia boards are run through a jointer to flatten sides that may have shifted when being clamped together.

Marking leg pieces to be cut to length. We used a miter saw.

## CUT THE MORTISES AND TENONS

Cut the base pieces to length. The legs are 29 inches (73.5 cm) long, the crosspieces are 23 inches (58.5 cm) long, and the stretcher is 48 inches (122 cm) long. The pieces will be held together by mortise and tenon joints, so figure the length of the tenons into the length the crosspieces and stretchers.

A similar router table setup for cutting tenons

Cutting leg mortises on a router table with a stop block. Notice that the mortise is open through the top of the joint.

## MORTISE AND TENON JOINTS

Simple, versatile, and strong, mortise and tenon joints are fundamental woodworking joints. One board has a mortise hole, and the other has a matching tenon tongue, which is inserted into the mortise and glued in place. Sometimes, additional support will be given by also adding a wood pin through the side of the joint.

Cut mortises in the top of each table leg

Using a plunge router to cut mortises

## THERE ARE TWO TYPES OF PEOPLE

Silas tells me that there are two types of people—those who round their tenons and others who square their mortises. We're working in Silas' workshop, so I feel obligated to choose Team Round Tenons.

Properly cut, but not perfect mortises. No worries. If you don't take a picture of them and put them in a book, no one will ever know what yours looked like.

The tenons are 1 inch (2.5 cm) wide and 1 1/2 inches (4 cm) long on the crosspieces and 1-inch (2.5 cm) long for the stretcher. On a router table, set the fence for the final length of the tenon and take multiple passes to cut the correct width. Use a saw to cut the back of the tenon and a chisel to round the length of the tenon. Use the router in a plunge base to cut the mortises. If the leg pieces aren't long enough to use a self-centering jig, you can set up a straight edge on your work stable and cut the mortises. We did opt to blow out the top of the mortises on our legs. This means our leg tenons can be a little taller.

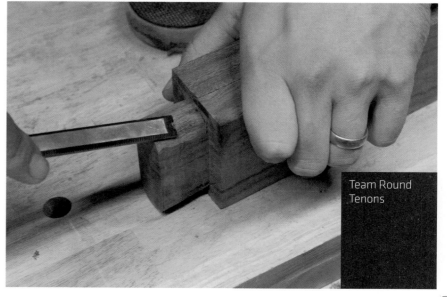

Team Round Tenons

Dry fitting the legs and crosspieces

Cutting the inside taper on each table leg

## DRY-FIT THE BASE JOINERY

Dry-fit all the joints to make sure they fit snugly. Drill holes through each end of the crosspieces into the stretcher and in each leg through the outside of the leg into the crosspiece for hardware. Adding hardware to the joinery adds extra strength and helps to make the base rock-solid. Use two bolts from the crosspieces into the stretcher and screws from the legs into the crosspieces. Use a Forstner bit to countersink the screws and be sure to drill a pilot hole all the way into both pieces. After assembly, glue in dowels to cover the screw holes and cut flush.

First stage of our multistage hardware holes

Drilling pilot holes through both pieces of wood

Gluing a leg to a crosspiece

Adding the screws that will help tighten up our joinery

## ROUGH SAND AND GLUE THE BASE

Before gluing all the base pieces together, give all the pieces a rough sanding. There are plenty of surfaces that will be harder to reach once your table base is glued together, so make the most of this opportunity to rough sand. To assemble, cover all sides of the tenons with a thin layer of glue and cover the inside of the mortise in glue as well (a small brush works well). The face around the mortise and the shoulder of the tenon do not need glue. They'll end up with glue from the joint, and starting with those faces glue-free will help minimize squeeze out in hard to sand places. Once the joints are glued and pulled together, drive in the hardware. Use firm pressure to tighten the bolts and screws but do not overtighten. Because of the hardware, there's no need for clamps while the glue dries.

A leg joint from the top

Drilling hole through the joined base to attach the top from underneath

Hardware for attaching table top to base

The woodworking store sanded both sides of the top at 80-grit. We'll use a hand sander to get it smooth.

## OPTIONAL STEP: CUT A TAPER FOR THE LEGS

I've chosen a tapered look for my legs, so now that my tenons are cut, it's a good idea to cut the taper on each leg. A track saw is a great tool for this sort of cut. It's important to choose the right moment to make a cut like this. Having square sides to a piece makes saws, drills, routers and even some sanders easier to use. You want to cut an angle like this at the last convenient step in the process.

## FINAL SANDING

Sand with 120-grit sandpaper and a small orbital sander. Sand all the parts of the base, even though it is joined together, if that's possible (depending on your base design). Make sure to think ahead about how you'll sand each piece.

Wiping on a polyurethane gel finish

## STEP 11

### APPLY THE FINISH

Finish with a polyurethane gel. This finish is very easy to apply and very forgiving when it comes to lap marks. With multiple coats, it's a strong and durable finish. This rub-in poly gel is best applied with a cotton cloth. First, wipe on a heavy coat. Then, wipe the excess off and buff the surface. That's best done with three separate cloths. Even though the gel is forgiving, you'll still want to have all your materials staged nearby so that you can work quickly.

## TAKE A MOMENT

At this point in the project, it's a little hard to get work done. I just want to stand around and admire the beautiful wood. It's amazing that these boards came from logs that were destined for the landfill. It's okay to take a moment to appreciate how the piece is coming together.

## ATTACH THE TOP AND ADD ANY FINAL TOUCHES

When the multiple coats of the finish dry, attach the top to the base. It's easiest to move the two pieces separately and attach them in the room. Use a similar system as the leg hardware to attach the two pieces, include a wide countersunk hole and a long pilot hole for the screw. Drill a slightly larger hole in the base than the bolt needs. That will allow the bolt to slide laterally as the top breathes. Use a ratchet to tighten the bolt just until it gives stiff resistance.

This handsome table is ready for anything my growing family can throw at it. It's not large, but it'll comfortably seat six.

Profile of dining table

Detail of tapered top

A dinner table is a rite of passage for any woodworker. I'm proud of my first table and not because it's the perfect design or even perfect execution. I'm proud because of what it means to my family. You'll never get as much use or as many compliments on a piece of furniture as your dinner table. If you use solid wood, strong joints, and care, a good table will last for generations. Wood that was once considered trash becomes a work of art to pass down to the next generation. When we care not just about the end product but also the materials and techniques that make them, we create true beauty.

PART FOUR
# FIREWOOD

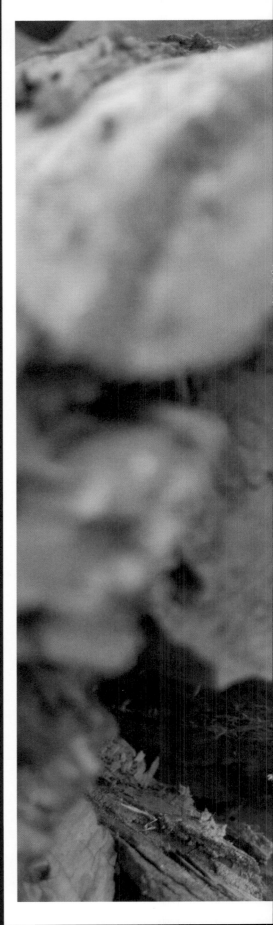

# CHOPPING FIREWOOD

Unfortunately, not every log is destined to become fine furniture, and that is okay. Generally, wood above the point a tree trunk splits into multiple branches is not suitable for milling into lumber, and many trees are too twisted or curved to be easily milled. A single tree can yield a huge amount of material, and since much of that can't be milled, firewood is a great way to divert waste from our landfills.

One of the most important and functional technologies humankind first mastered was fire. Nowadays, most homes aren't primarily warmed by wood-burning stoves, but there's not much that's better than sitting by a campfire on a chilly winter night. Having a handy supply of well-seasoned firewood that you chopped and stacked yourself can be gratifying and can even save you a bundle of money. The process for high quality firewood is not complicated. In this section, we cover proper chopping, stacking, and seasoning.

Two considerations are important when sizing your firewood: length and width. Length is determined by the size of your fireplace or an average campfire; proper width is crucial for the seasoning process and for even burning.

Splitting wide logs is easier using a wedge.

Using an axe to split firewood

Begin the process by using a chainsaw to cut or buck the wood into approximately 16-inch (40.5 cm) lengths. This is a convenient length that fits into most any fireplace or wood-burning stove. Keep one of the ends of log propped up and secured to keep your chain from contacting the ground. Make sure you leave a couple extra inches (5 cm) hanging beyond your prop to make sure things don't shift at the end of your cut. Clean perpendicular cuts will ensure that the log doesn't tip over in the next step.

## TOOLS

Chainsaw

Axe or splitting maul

Splitting wedge

Small sledge hammer

Splitting wedge

A proper swing will leave your arms fully extended. This helps the axe head travel as fast as possible and keeps you away from the blade.

Even with a small sledge hammer, wedges are often the best way to split small amounts of firewood.

Eucalyptus can be very beautiful. If I had gotten to this log before it was bucked into small pieces, it could have been so much more.

Once the wood is bucked, it's time to split it into firewood. There are some nuances and tricks that will make the process easier and safer. Sometimes, older axes have loose heads, so make sure the axe head is secure. The last thing you want is to send that head flying wildly through the air. Use a large stump to serve as the platform where you'll stand the pieces to be chopped. Check for irregularities in the wood, such as where a small branch came out, and put that side closer to the ground. The goal is to begin the split with the straightest grain possible. Before taking a swing, scope out where you plan on striking with the axe head, making note of any large cracks already present. It's best to start by halving the log and then taking slices out of the halves like a pie. The larger the log, the more slices you'll need. Try not to let the slices go over 6 inches (15 cm) in width. Bigger than that, and the wood will take longer to season and will be harder to light.

A proper swing will take the axe or maul in a long arching motion. Make sure that your arm becomes fully extended and gets the splitting head as high as possible. Place yourself in a position that keeps your feet safe from the axe head if you miss your mark and hit a glancing blow. After a few minutes of chopping, you will understand why; swinging an axe can be very tiring, and the more you let gravity do the work, the more efficient you will be. The goal is not to cut the wood, but to split it, using the axe as a wedge. Splitting mauls are made specifically for the task as they have a wider edge that will push the two sides apart further, splitting wood more quickly.

For wider logs, or the more difficult ones, you should have a splitting wedge and sledgehammer handy. The process is much the same as the splitting we covered back in the milling sections, but without the need of multiple wedges due the shorter length of the logs. You will occasionally encounter pieces that never quite split the way you want them to and that's okay. As long as you're being smart and safe, you'll end up with something that'll burn.

Overall, there are not many exercises that will get your blood moving better than a good wood chopping session, and the process can be oddly peaceful.

# STACKING FIREWOOD

A small stack of firewood from limbs trimmed off a backyard eucalyptus tree

Compared to stacking lumber, firewood is easy. You don't have to worry about warping or a dead-flat foundation, though for a stable pile, you will want a fairly even surface to start with. There are some pretty involved approaches to firewood stacking, but I prefer a simple but effective method.

Choose a location with good drainage that doesn't flood with rain. If you get a lot of rain, put the pile under shelter or put an old piece of corrugated roofing or such on top of the stack to keep the rain off. The foundation can be built up similarly to a lumber pile, using cinderblocks or treated wood to elevate the pile off the ground. These steps will prevent the wood from rotting. Stacking green firewood indoors is not a good idea. Remember that green wood can contain more than its dry weight in water; as it dries, a stack will release hundreds of pounds of water into the air.

Flat stacks

Stack the wood loosely, with plenty of small gaps between the pieces. If need be, you can stack a layer crossways to keep the pile stable. Keep the pile from falling apart by using vertical posts on either end. The key to a good firewood stack is airflow. Remember back in the seasoning lumber section? Firewood is no different; it needs airflow to wick off the moisture. If you need to stack your wood two rows deep, make sure you put a gap between the stacks so that air can move freely around both.

Seasoning firewood properly takes 6 to 12 months depending on the climate. Oftentimes, people begin building up their wood piles in spring so that by wintertime they have properly seasoned firewood. Ensuring that your wood is dry will maximize the efficiency of your fire. Too wet, and it will be harder to start and emit less heat and more smoke. The target moisture is around 20 percent moisture content. If you aren't sure how dry the wood is, use a moisture meter like you did when seasoning your lumber.

Seasoning firewood isn't hard, but foresight and patience are needed. Plan ahead for your firewood needs and get that wood chopped up and stacked in plenty of time to properly season.

A simple foundation made from concrete bricks and landscape timber. I even had the home store cut the timber for me so it was easier to transport.

Stacked firewood

Stacked firewood

PART FIVE
# THE LEFTOVERS

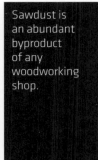

Sawdust is an abundant byproduct of any woodworking shop.

## SAWDUST NO-NO

Do not use walnut, butternut, or beech sawdust for animal bedding or mulching. These trees produce a chemical called juglone, which can cause irritation and may stunt plant growth.

If you work with raw wood long enough, you will find that a good chunk of any given log never makes it into your prized creation, instead becoming wood chips, sawdust, and cut-offs. The more you build, the more waste you generate, and it can quickly become a nuisance. What are you supposed to do with all the leftovers? In my small shop, I don't have space to save all the cut-offs, and dumping large bags of sawdust in the garbage is messy and a waste.

Thankfully, there are loads of creative ways to use sawdust and woodchips in a productive way that extends the usefulness of the tree. The material is organic, absorbent, insulating, fibrous, and flammable—all properties which make it versatile. Since the options are endless, we've decided to tell you about some especially useful applications helpful around the home and yard.

# ANIMAL BEDDING

Sawdust has its uses for owners of pets or livestock, foremost of which is bedding. David and I both keep backyard chickens, which are a great way to dispose of food scraps, and which yield eggs and organic garden fertilizer. Wood shavings are always in use, providing a nice soft floor to their nesting boxes. If you've ever had hamsters or gerbils, you've probably found yourself buying sawdust shavings from the store or shredding old newspapers for the bedding in their cages. Even large animals such as horses have need of something to soften their homes.

When using sawdust with animals, keep in mind that not all sawdust is suitable. Very fine dust is best avoided, as it can cause respiratory problems. Instead, use larger shavings, like those that come off a planer. Chainsaw mills also put off some nice, coarse shavings. This makes for a comfortable bed and keeps down the irritating dust.

Some species of woods, like walnut, can cause more serious health problems to animals, so in general, be conservative with what you use near your beloved animal friends. For the most part, avoid hardwoods for such uses and save your pine, cedar, fir, and other softwood shavings for the animals.

Silas' backyard chicken house

A curious Buff Orpington hen peeking out the door

A fresh bed of pine wood shavings in the laying boxes

# MULCH

Wood is an organic matter, so mulching is a great use for sawdust. Since it absorbs water like a sponge, sawdust mulch helps keep the soil nice and moist underneath, and its insulating properties help protect tree roots against extreme temperature swings.

Beyond physical properties, it can help add to the diversity and quantity of organisms in your soil as it breaks down, which is a good thing for plants. The benefits from sawdust mulching are typically long term, and I've not had as much success with them in the garden, which has a limited season before turnover, so I like to use it for young trees as they are getting established. Seeing a new tree prosper with the help of the remains from an old fallen tree offers a sense of harmony, don't you think?

Silas spreads a layer of sawdust mulch around a young peach tree.

## STEP 1

### CLEAR THE MULCHING AREA

Around the tree you are going to mulch, clear an area around the trunk, as wide as the tree's canopy. Create a basin a couple inches (5 cm) lower than ground level to keep the mulch from spreading and to act as a retention basin when watering.

Clearing the area and adding chicken manure

Sawdust is raked evenly around the tree bed.

## STEP 2

### ADD NITROGEN

Wood is very high in carbon, which is essential for plants, but when out of balance with the other ingredients necessary for good soil, it can be a showstopper. To compensate, add nitrogen to the soil where the mulch is to be applied. This will help the sawdust to break down and begin adding more and more nutritional benefits to the soil. Some good organic sources of nitrogen are blood meal, composted chicken manure, or fish meal.

## STEP 3

### ADD SAWDUST

Layer the sawdust in your retention basin a couple inches (5 cm) thick, resting above the soil. Because the wood is so high in carbon—and can also cause the soil's acidity to spike up while it breaks down—don't incorporate the sawdust into the soil. It's a good idea to leave a couple inches (5 cm) of a buffer between the mulch and the tree trunk to avoid rot, which can be encouraged by the constant moisture retained by the sawdust.

This thick layer of sawdust mulch will help retain moisture and regulate heat, and as it breaks down, it will naturally incorporate itself into the soil.

A large bag of sawdust

# GARDEN PATHWAY COVER

A practical use for sawdust in the garden is as a cover for your pathways. You've got to have space to work between rows, and when they get wet, paths can get muddy. Adding a layer of sawdust and woodchips mixed together on the surface will help avoid this problem.

Be careful to keep the sawdust contained to the path as sawdust mixed with soil can drain it of nitrogen. Lining the path with stones or bricks will keep the material from spilling over into the garden bed and will add a nice visual element to your garden. Before too long, the sawdust will begin to break down into organic material and a new layer will be needed.

David rakes a fresh layer of sawdust on the garden path.

The first layer of wood chips is laid.

Sawdust is spread over the wood chips.

A finished garden path

The mixture is raked together evenly across the path.

# FIRE STARTERS

Sawdust burns very well—maybe too well, in fact. Paired with a catalyst like wax, it can be used in place of large amounts of tinder to start a fire. We'll be putting sawdust in small paper cups and then melting wax over the top to create a durable and waterproof fire starter.

Firestarters made from sawdust

All the components ready to be mixed

Cupcake cups about half filled with sawdust

A layer of wax is added over the sawdust.

## STEP 1
### FILL THE CUPS

Cover a metal baking sheet with parchment paper. This helps keep any excess wax from sticking to your pan. Arrange plain paper cupcake cups on the pan, leaving an inch or so (2.5 cm) of space between each. Fill each cup about half of the way full with sawdust. A mix of dust and small planer chips works best.

## STEP 2
### ADD THE WAX

Use wax chips to cover the sawdust in each cup. A mixture of two parts sawdust and one part wax works best. The primary fuel is the wood; the wax is only a catalyst to keep the wood burning longer and to bind the sawdust together. Too much wax and the fire starters will burn too slowly. The whole mission of a fire starter is to burn very hot so that you can catch large pieces of wood quickly. Experiment with different mixtures to find the best ratio for your sawdust.

## MATERIALS

Sawdust

Soy wax

Paper cupcake cups

**TIP**

One of the advantages of using paper cups is that you can easily get things started by lighting the exposed paper.

### STEP 3

### BAKE

Place the baking sheet in 350° (180°C, or gas mark 4) oven until the wax has melted. Do not leave them unattended because it takes just a few minutes. The sawdust to wax ratio you use will determine your melting time. Once the wax has melted, remove from the oven and let cool. You should end up with small little pucks of sawdust that pack a big punch.

Before they can make fire, they must bake.

Lighting up a fire starter

A crackling fire quickly emerges

# ACKNOWLEDGMENTS

**Thanks to...**

Our families for their patience, support, and always helping us achieve our goals.

Our parents and siblings for helping us to become who we are.

Wine Glass Bar Saw Mill for their generosity with their time and resources.

Redemption Church for caring about our city.

Todd Langford

Ty Moser

George Pongracz

Sam Sherrill

Evan Shively

Norm Abram

Russell Morash

David Blakeman

# ABOUT THE AUTHORS

**Silas Kyler** is an Arizona native and resides in Tempe, Arizona, with his wife and three young children. Having graduated from Scottsdale Community College with an associate's degree in film production, Silas has always had an interest in telling stories through film and took inspiration from what people were doing with urban lumber for *Felled*, his first feature length documentary. For as long as he can remember, Silas has enjoyed building things with his hands. Woodworking has been a hobby of his throughout his adult life, and his passion for urban lumber was a driving force behind *The Art and Craft of Wood*.

**David Hildreth** is a documentary filmmaker who lives in Tempe, Arizona, with his wife and daughter. He starting making videos with his friends in junior high school and never stopped. After learning about the fate of many trees that blow down in monsoon storms and the passion with which people are using them for art, he knew he wanted to help raise awareness of urban lumber. *Felled* and *The Art and Craft of Wood* are two ways he has been blessed to create culture and spread the message that everything, even garbage, can be beautiful.

# INDEX

# ALSO AVAILABLE

## Building with Secondhand Stuff
978-1-58923-662-2

## The Organic Artist
978-1-59253-926-0

## The Backyard Blacksmith
978-1-59253-251-3

## How to Weld
978-0-76033-174-3